PRESENTED TO:

_____

BY:

_____

DATE:

_____

SEASONS
OF LIFE

*Reflections to Celebrate
the Heart of a Woman*

Karen Hardin

WHITE STONE BOOKS
LAKELAND, FLORIDA

*Unless otherwise noted as an excerpt from previously published articles,
all interviews were conducted by and manuscript written by
Karen Hardin in conjunction with White Stone Books, Inc.*

07 06 05 04   10 9 8 7 6 5 4 3 2 1

Seasons of Life:
Reflections to Celebrate the Heart of a Woman
ISBN 1-59379-011-2
Copyright © 2004 by Karen Hardin
P. O. Box 700515
Tulsa, Oklahoma 74170-0515

Published by White Stone Books, Inc.
P. O. Box 2835
Lakeland, Florida 33806

Project Editor: Betsy Williams, williams.services.inc@cox.net

ACKNOWLEDGMENTS

With special thanks:

To Betsy Williams, your friendship and your prayers have been an anchor for me throughout this project. Without your encouragement, I might never have started.

To Linda Overton, you never cease to amaze me. Thank you for being my cheerleader.

To Keith Provance, thank you for believing in me. Your leadership has impacted my life more than you know.

To all the ladies who let me write your stories. This is *your* book.

To Mom, thank you for all the times you dropped everything to help with the kids, so I could have time to do another interview or write. You are amazing.

To my wonderful husband, Kevin, thank you for your prayers, your patience, and your enduring love during this difficult schedule. I love you.

Contents

To everything there is a season,
A time for every purpose under heaven.

ECCLESIASTES 3:1 NKJV

INTRODUCTION

The doorbell rang. I made a quick glance around the room as I headed to the door. What a mess. Toys were scattered across the floor, a sheet was wadded up in the corner from the "tent" we had made earlier, and my throw pillows, which had been transformed into stepping-stones, lined a path from the sofa to the now defunct tent.

I shook my head and swallowed my pride as I opened the door, wondering if I would ever have a clean house again or time of my own. With three children ages seven, four, and two, there seemed very little time during the day—no matter how hard I tried—to accomplish tasks of my own choosing.

As I opened the door, my mind switched to the old saying, "If you came to see me, come on in. If you came to see my house, you'd better come back later." Fortunately, it was my friend, Teri. She would graciously ignore my house.

Sensing my frustration, Teri began to encourage me. With three of her four kids already in their teens, she smiled with compassion. "It's only a season, Karen. Seasons change as your children grow. Then they'll need your time in other ways," she said with a knowing smile. She was now in what I refer to as the "chauffeur years," driving her kids back and forth to numerous sports and church activities on a constant basis. Her life was just as busy as mine, only in a different way.

When asked how he successfully dealt with retirement from the military and his previously regimented lifestyle, General Norman Schwarzkopf, Commander-in-Chief, Central Command of the Gulf War, replied, "I've learned that life is a collection of seasons."

What season of life are you in?

Each of us will walk through a variety of seasons in our lives. Whether it is from teen to young adult or senior to a woman in her sunset years, seasons are an unchangeable fact of life, each with its share of blessings and challenges. You may not be able to change what season you are in, but you can change how you walk through it. We've all seen or heard of people who have walked through the most horrendous events imaginable, yet somehow have come through stronger. (See Lisa Beamer's story, page 138.) On the other hand, there are those who progress through life in terms of years, but carry the baggage of failure, rejection, and pain from one season to the next. Which will you choose to do?

How we transition is also important. Too often people make the mistake of trying to hold on to a season of life that is now past. We can liken it to a star athlete who is physically past his prime. He must decide whether to prolong his "season of glory," which will ultimately result in failure, or graciously take the success he has gained and use it to his advantage. For him, this could mean retirement as well as unlimited opportunities for new adventures and growth. But the blessings of the next season are hindered until he lets go of the past.

On the other hand, there are those who strive to exit their present season, in order to enter the next one, assuming it will provide greener pastures. Although God is not the cause of difficult seasons, He is with us in the midst of them and can use them to develop a deeper maturity and strength in us when we turn our struggle over to Him. The key is to recognize and appreciate God's blessings right where you are, making the most of every single day.

Finally, circumstances can determine seasons as well. While some of these seasons are a joy, others may be thrust upon us against our will. Whatever the case, it is necessary to remember that each season is simply that—a season. It is temporary. So whether you are going through a healing process or the aging process, with God's help you will one day move on.

As you read this book, I encourage you to evaluate your present situation and work toward these goals:

- Recognize the season you are in.

- Accept where you are, and use it to your advantage.

- Discover the blessings in your present season and treasure them.

- Take the successes and wisdom from past seasons, and bring them into your present one.

- Leave the failures of the past behind.

Most important of all, as you walk through this season and the ones to come, remember:

He has made everything beautiful in its time.

ECCLESIASTES 3:11

The Promise of

Spring

YOUNG SINGLE

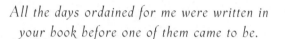

Alisa Girard

OF ZOEGIRL
(AS TOLD TO KAREN HARDIN)

*All the days ordained for me were written in
your book before one of them came to be.*

PSALM 139:16

I was twenty-three before I had my first kiss. And you
know what? After it happened, I wished I had waited longer!

From an early age, I prayed that my first boyfriend would
be my husband. Although it didn't work out that way, my moti-
vation was sincere. I told God that I didn't want to waste my
time dating guys who weren't for me. That was my intention at
least. But it hasn't been easy to follow through on that decision,
and there are times that, I have to admit, I haven't followed my
own advice.

One such instance was when I began dating a guy who was
really nice, but very domineering. I knew he wasn't for me, but

we had fun together; so the relationship continued. I soon learned the hard way that guys like that tend to make a girl feel like she is nothing—that she should somehow feel lucky just to have him in her life. It took me awhile, but I got out of that relationship before it could further erode my self-confidence.

Another instance that was difficult was when a couple of my friends, who were younger than I, got married right out of high school. While I was happy for them, my immediate response was, "God, I've been faithful! Where's *my* husband?"

I know I am not the only one who has asked that question. As we in ZOEgirl have traveled from city to city, I've talked to many girls who say, "I feel like a loser because I've never been kissed." They long for what they feel is a "seal of approval" on their lives. But our seal of approval doesn't come from being accepted by a man; it comes from our relationship with God.

Today's immoral society does not hold sacred purity before marriage, but God has given us that standard for our protection. Before that first kiss, it is so much easier to stand up to the pressures of temptation that can follow.

There have been moments in which my singleness has created a deep loneliness. But it has also been through these times of solitude that God has taught me the power of who He really is. I am grateful that these experiences have allowed me to grow in who I am and who He wants me to be.

We all crave affection, the desire to be hugged and held by another person.

But I've learned that God is able to hold me, in a spiritual sense, and comfort me. I've learned the importance of letting Him hold me during these vulnerable times and not seeking the arms of the "wrong" one. I know He'll bring the man He's chosen for me at just the right time.

As of press time, there has been an exciting conclusion to Alisa's story. She has gotten married! After four years of friendship, her relationship with ZOEgirl's musical director and drummer, Mike Childers, turned more serious, and they tied the knot this past summer. Of the marriage Alisa shares, "I am so happy and fulfilled with my new life. I feel as if everything up until now has led up to this moment. My heart has finally come home."

Dear God, it must make You sad when I think I have to have a boyfriend to feel like I have value. Jesus paid the ultimate price for me, so because of that I know I'm greatly loved and valuable to You. I trust You with the whole issue of my singleness, knowing You have my life in the palm of Your hand. Amen.

ALISA GIRARD, part of the dynamic trio ZOEgirl, and her husband, Mike Childers, live in Franklin, Tennessee, with their two cats, Butler and Baxter.

POPULARITY AT ALL COST

Lisa

*Do you not know that your body is a
temple of the Holy Spirit, who is in you,
whom you have received from God?*

1 CORINTHIANS 6:19

I loved being popular and was willing to do whatever it took to stay that way. I was the self-dubbed "Queen of Peer Pressure" as I allowed it to mold almost every decision I made. This intense need for approval had a profound effect on my life until I was in my early twenties.

I came from a middle-class home with loving and caring parents and an older sister and brother. Unfortunately, ours was what has become typical in America, a family in which Christianity is professed, but with little outward evidence. The only times I attended church during these formative years was when my grandmother or school friends took me, receiving little or no spiritual instruction at home.

While I had an inner but unrecognized longing for the Lord, my social status was the most important factor in my life at that time. My self-worth came in the form of a date, which was a necessary requirement each weekend on my social calendar. The few times I didn't have a date, I went out cruising town with my friends. To stay home meant certain death to my popularity, at least in my mind.

If there was a party, I was there and gradually began experimenting with drinking. Fortunately, drinking never became a stronghold in my life as I had already seen the devastating effects of alcohol in my own family. But guys were another story.

When you play with fire, you eventually get burned. Just because I had a date didn't mean I had sex, but with the guys I dated for any length of time, we eventually went down a road I never intended to go.

After college my life became a strange paradox of weekend nightclub visits, followed by dutiful Sunday church attendance. This pattern continued until finally an emptiness I could no longer ignore filled my heart. *There has to be more to life than what I've experienced so far,* I thought to myself.

Determined to see a change, the very next Sunday my best friend and I attended a different church nearby. Even as I sat in the unfamiliar surroundings, I felt a strange sense of belonging as the message stirred my heart. It was the first time I had really heard and understood the message of

Christ's sacrifice for my sin. My life changed immediately as I gave my heart to the Lord.

I was now motivated to read my Bible, and it was making sense. As my relationship with God deepened, I no longer had a compelling need to drink or party, and I had no desire for sex outside of marriage. It was a powerful thing that I now found my self-worth in my relationship with God. The "love" from the opposite sex, which had always been a compelling need in my life, was no longer necessary. For the first time in my life, I was completely content alone.

My newfound relationship with the Lord continued to deepen as I committed every area to God's control, including my previously all-important social life. The incredible change that took place surprised even me.

God, I don't want to do this dating thing, I remember crying out to Him after going on a date with a Christian man several weeks later. The evening had been awkward. I hadn't even wanted to go out, and I surely didn't know the rules for "Christian" dating. As the evening came to a close, I had no idea what to do, but I knew it wasn't what I had done before. So I gave my date a quick hug and said good night.

I made a pledge to God that very night, "I just want it to be You and me, God. I don't care if I ever date again until You bring the man You have for me." God knew that I meant what I had said and that I was willing to wait as long as necessary. What I didn't realize was that in making that decision and turning the keys of my heart over to God, I had set into motion

His ultimate plan for my life. I discovered that as I relinquished all rights to guide my own life, God was then able to bring about something far greater than I could have ever dreamed.

The very next day after I prayed that prayer of consecration, I met the man who would later become my husband! It didn't take long once I decided to do things God's way and in His timing.

Dear God, I want to keep my eyes and my heart completely on You. Help me find my self-worth in You and to come to know Your incredible love for me on a personal basis. Help me not to be drawn into the ways of the world, but to live pure and holy before You. Amen.

A DANGEROUS GAME: TAKING MATTERS INTO YOUR OWN HANDS

Karen Hardin

*Delight yourself in the LORD and he will give
you the desires of your heart. Commit your way
to the LORD; trust in him and he will do this.*

PSALM 37:4–5

"Carrie" longed to be married. In fact, it was all she had dreamed about, but now it was slowly turning from a dream to an obsession.

Although she was only twenty-seven, most of her close friends were married, many already with children. Feeling the mounting pressure from society, she made the fateful decision that rather than waiting for God's timing, she would plunge ahead with her own plan to achieve her goal of matrimony.

Calculatingly, Carrie chose one of the single unattached men who worked in the same building as she. She began to write the handsome young man letters requesting help in one area or another. At first the letters were accepted and assistance offered, but as the appeals increased and the true nature of her intent became apparent, the young man completely cut off further contact.

Undeterred, Carrie set her sites on another potential suitor and began with a similar approach only to be rejected again once her true motive became clear. Finally, she chose yet another eligible bachelor and this time another method. She chose a close girlfriend, one who already had a steady boyfriend, to accompany her in her scheme. With her "safe" friend in tow, she arranged chance meetings with her new prospective husband. Once a friendship began to develop, she arranged outings and several "chance" meetings for the three-some. But this time her plotting backfired as the young man eventually fell in love with and married the very girlfriend Carrie had brought along as "safe."

Feelings of betrayal now became mixed with mounting feel-ings of rejection. It was an all-consuming drive that birthed bizarre and manipulative behavior until finally Carrie was placed in a mental institution.

Singleness is not a disease or a curse. In actuality, it is an opportunity that can bring both growth and adven-ture. In fact, many married people reflect on their single days, wishing they had done more to live those days to the fullest. Singles have considerably more time to pursue hobbies, higher education, career goals, and their relationship with God. When marriage becomes the ultimate goal in a single person's life, it can result in frustration and unhealthy relationships that, even when they do lead to marriage, too often end in divorce.

Marriage is not a line that once crossed signals the beginning of life. It is simply another season—although an important one—in the lives of many. Don't put your life on hold until you meet Mr. Right. Instead, let God guide your dreams and pursuits, and ultimately, His road will take you to fulfillment that can include Mr. Right at just the right time.

Dear God, help me to focus my attention on becoming the person You want me to be rather than trying to find a person whom I think will add meaning to my life. Give me patience to wait on You, grow in You, and know You more. And if Your plan for me includes marriage, I trust You to bring the right man at the right time. Amen.

WOMEN OF THE BIBLE
Rebekah[1]

*Your beauty should not come from outward adornment, such
as braided hair and the wearing of gold jewelry and fine
clothes. Instead, it should be that of your inner self, the unfad-
ing beauty of a gentle and quiet spirit, which is of great worth
in God's sight. For this is the way holy women of the past who
put their hope in God used to make themselves beautiful.*

1 PETER 3:3–5

"O LORD, God of my master Abraham, give me success
today, and show kindness to my master Abraham" (Gen. 24:12),
prayed the servant whom Abraham commanded to go to their
homeland to obtain a wife for Abraham's son Isaac.

The servant's prayer was specific, "See, I am standing
beside this spring, and the daughters of the townspeople are
coming out to draw water. May it be that when I say to a girl,
'Please let down your jar that I may have a drink,' and she says,
'Drink, and I'll water your camels too'—let her be the one you
have chosen for your servant Isaac" (Gen. 24:13–14).

Abraham, through his servant, was looking for an excep-
tional bride for his son Isaac. What would set her apart?
Rebekah is described as "very beautiful and a virgin" (v. 16), but
she also had another important virtue ... kindness. When the
servant asked for a drink, she readily honored his request and
voluntarily offered to draw water for his camels.

---

[1] See Genesis 24.

Have you ever considered this task she committed herself to? How much water would a camel who had just crossed the desert need? How many camels did the servant have? Jar after jar of water would have to be lowered to the bottom of the deep well, pulled slowly back up, and then carried to the watering trough. It was time–consuming, heavy work, inconvenient at best. But it was a task done from the heart for a stranger in need with no thought of reward for herself.

Of course this was all part of God's divine plan, and His plans include blessing for everyone involved. He granted Abraham's request for a wife for his son; He answered the servant's prayer; He blessed Isaac with a beautiful wife; and He richly rewarded Rebekah for her graciousness.

The actions of the heart are what bring distinction to our lives. Purity, especially in our present society, is a treasure indeed. What sets you apart?

Dear Father, I want to be a godly and gracious woman like Rebekah. Let my beauty begin first in my heart and then express itself in my demeanor and actions toward others. Most of all, I want to be beautiful in Your sight. Amen.

LIFE'S LESSON

1. Develop the fruit of kindness in your life—being readily willing to help others, even when it's inconvenient.
2. Remain pure in spirit, soul, and body; and seek cleansing and forgiveness should you slip.
3. Let your actions and your appearance be reflections of your true inner beauty.

ENGAGEMENT

*K*ristin *S*winford

OF ZOE*GIRL*

(AS TOLD TO KAREN HARDIN)

> *Plans fail for lack of counsel, but*
> *with many advisers they succeed.*

PROVERBS 15:22

"Prepare for the marriage and not just the wedding," the pastor encouraged us during one of our premarital counseling sessions, and thanks to him, we were fully aware of the commitment we were making to one another. It was the best advice he could have given. The wedding did have to be planned, however, and up to that point it hadn't been easy. I never realized how time-consuming and stressful it could be in just the planning stage, but even this process continued to bring us closer together.

Ryan and I met while attending the same high school in Jackson, Missouri, when he was a junior and I a sophomore.

We were both in Chamber Choir, but never had a date until my best friend and her brother, Ryan's best friend, schemed to bring us together.

We not only became a couple, but we also grew to be best friends as we dated through the remainder of high school, attending church, football games, and our proms. But as often happens in the relationships of youth, it didn't withstand the transition of graduation and college and resulted in our eventual breakup. Our relationship continued in an on-again/off-again fashion until finally we made the decision to separate, so we could seek God's will regarding it. This was not an easy decision, and I finally had to face the fact that Ryan and I might never be together again.

These breakups were painful, yet they provided an excellent opportunity for growth and maturity in both of our lives. And although Ryan's and my future together remained uncertain, my relationship with God reached a deeper and stronger level than ever before. It was during this time that ZOEgirl was formed.

I've always loved to sing, but it wasn't until I was a senior in high school that I realized what an important influence this love would play in my future. During that time, I attended a youth retreat in Texas. It was a huge gathering of around twenty-eight thousand people. Several well-known artists were featured, and it was an anointed time of worship. As Crystal Lewis stepped onstage and began to sing, it was as if a lightbulb was suddenly turned on in my heart and I heard God speak to me, *This is why I gave you the gift to sing.* I continued to pursue this passion in college, and it wasn't long afterwards that ZOEgirl was formed.

Around the same time that our first album was about to be released, Ryan and I got back into contact again. He began calling, tentatively at first, cautiously testing the waters as we reentered each other's lives. As the phone conversations lengthened, we finally decided that he should come to Nashville—where I had moved to pursue my music—for the weekend. It was time to see, once and for all, what was to be the destiny of our relationship.

Prior to his arrival, I spent a lot of time in prayer. We had been through this so many times before. I wanted to know for sure if he was the one God had for me. The second I opened the door, I knew in my heart as I saw him standing there, once again looking into his beautiful boyish blue eyes that had captured my heart so many years ago. I learned that during our separation, Ryan had also come into a new place with his relationship with God. It was as if God needed that time with both of us individually—not as a couple—to show us His plan, His timing, and His will for both of our lives.

Four months later, Ryan moved to Nashville and the relationship grew more serious. But the strength of our relationship was about to be tested once again. One week after Ryan arrived, I left on my first tour with ZOEgirl. He had just moved into an apartment by himself, in a new city where he knew only a handful of people. He stuck with it though, telling me often, "It's been hard to make Nashville my home, but this is where you are, so that's where I want to be."

In spite of these challenges, the relationship continued to progress. Ryan took my father to lunch shortly after arriving in Nashville to share with him his intention to pursue marriage with me. A little over a year later, Ryan took the engagement ring to my dad, asking for his blessing before he proposed. After nine years, it was finally our time and we became engaged.

Even during the engagement, we faced some unique challenges. Most of the wedding details had to be planned long distance while I was on the road! I am so thankful for wonderful friends and especially my mom who helped with this process. She is so organized—which I am not!

Thankfully, we followed our pastor's advice and planned for both the wedding and marriage. The time we invested in prayer, growing in our relationship with God and each other, and premarital counseling allowed us to talk through areas before they would become issues later. Our pastor gently helped us realize the strengths and weaknesses we both were bringing to the relationship, guiding us to see how these traits would affect our communication and very foundation.

Already we have faced challenges common for many couples. For example, within the first six months, Ryan's car was in need of major repair. At the time we wondered how we would pay for the added expense. But we are learning that these challenges can be easily overcome when we are committed to each other and to our relationship with God.

And while frequent separation is definitely the biggest challenge we have faced in our relationship due to my travel schedule for the group, Ryan has been 100 percent supportive. He has told me time and time again how he supports all that I do and takes pride in watching me get to fulfill my dream and calling. I couldn't ask for a more amazing and supportive husband!

Dear God, deciding whom to marry is one of the biggest decisions I will ever make. You know me better than I know myself, and I trust Your choice of a life mate for me. When the right time comes, help us to use wisdom as we progress in our relationship. Help us to build a firm foundation that we can build upon for the rest of our lives. Amen.

KRISTIN SWINFORD and her husband, Ryan, live in Nashville, Tennessee. They look forward to one day starting a family, but until then share their home with their dog Mazzy and two cats, Sadie and Sylvie.

WAS THIS THE MAN I WAS TO MARRY?

Sarah

Write the vision; make it plain on tablets, so that a runner may read it. For there is still a vision for the appointed time; it speaks of the end, and does not lie. If it seems to tarry, wait for it; it will surely come, it will not delay.

HABAKKUK 2:2–3 NRSV

I was just two weeks away from marrying the wrong person when the wedding was called off. Looking back it is hard to believe I came so close to missing God's best for me. Thankfully, by His grace, we were able to recognize the difficulties prior to walking down the aisle. Many couples are not so fortunate. Getting caught up in the excitement of being in love, planning the impending wedding, fearing failure, or fearing that Mr. Right will never come along, are just a few of the reasons that compel many to proceed in relationships. Some of these relationships however, if scrutinized would reveal the threads of commitment ready to unravel at the first sign of difficulty.

So what happens in dating relationships that can cause us to miss God's best? Many people used to tell me I was too picky. In my mind I had my "list" of things that were important to me and had vowed I would never marry anyone unless that important criteria was met. I'm not talking about superficial things such as looks or height, but weightier issues of the heart. For me it was a call to missions, and I knew that the man I would marry would have to share that calling. Somewhere along the way, I compromised this issue without even realizing it.

Marriage is one of the biggest crossroads in our lives—a major transition that will affect every other aspect of our future. Jeremiah 29:11 TLB shares God's heart for us: "I know the plans I have for you, says the Lord. They are plans for good and not for evil, to give you a future and a hope." God has a plan that is handcrafted specifically for each of us that utilizes our gifts, talents, and desires. The question is, are you willing to trust Him to bring that match that is perfect for you?

From a young age, I knew I was to reach the nations with the Gospel—especially the teens of these nations. Attending a Christian school, we were often given the opportunity to participate in short-term mission trips during our spring and summer breaks. I always participated in these events and would encourage as many classmates as possible to join us. I had no idea the impact this would have on my own future.

One of these trips was to Ghana, Africa. At that time I felt impressed to encourage Caleb, one of my classmates I had known since elementary school, to go. Caleb was one of the basketball stars in school. He was good-looking, popular, had a beautiful girlfriend, and was completely uninterested in missions. He did decide to join the mission trip, but for all the wrong reasons. He was looking for adventure! It turned into an adventure all right. Working and preaching in remote regions and seeing the mighty miracles of God changed not only the lives of the African people we worked with, but Caleb's heart as well.

It was during this trip that Caleb and I entered into an unusual conversation. I'm not sure what brought it up, but I told him about God's call on my life for ministry. I explained that because of my intense desire to serve and please God, I resolved early on that I would never even kiss a guy I was dating until the day I married. Little did I know that as Caleb heard those words, it sparked something inside him, and he said to himself, *I'm going to be that person.* It wasn't a romantic thing or even a conscious decision that he decided he wanted to marry me. It was something from deep inside that remained in his heart for the next seven years.

I didn't realize until later how much Caleb had changed as a result of that trip. Basketball was no longer his idol. God was now on the throne of his heart. He even turned down a basketball scholarship after sensing God's leading to attend a different university. After graduating from high school and quite independently, we decided to attend the same university. All the while Caleb continued to pray over the words birthed in his heart a couple of years before, *I'm going to be that person.* We were good friends, but in my heart, nothing more.

One day after Caleb attended an evangelistic meeting, he had a vision of the two of us ministering together around the world. In his heart this vision confirmed the word he had been praying over for the last several years. He was now convinced that we were to marry, but circumstances seemed to indicate otherwise as I began dating and later became engaged to a fellow student at the university. Caleb could have given up. Instead, however, he continued to pray, never saying a word regarding the vision or the thoughts of his heart. He gave the matter to God and rested in His plan and timing.

Even after my engagement was broken, Caleb wisely kept quiet, knowing I needed time to heal. It was another year and a half before he pursued a relationship with me. But within the first date or two, as he shared his heart and goals for the future, I knew immediately what a change had occurred in him since our high school days. I also knew that he was the man I was to marry. And unlike my previous engagement, this time everything fit perfectly.

Dear God, give me insight and wisdom so I can make the right decision regarding the man You have picked for me. Help me follow Your voice and not my emotions. Keep me from making wrong decisions that would bring painful results. Amen.

CALEB AND SARAH WEHRLI are teen mission directors for Victory Christian Center in Tulsa, Oklahoma.

PREPARATION OF THE HEART

Karen Hardin

*Unless the LORD builds the house,
its builders labor in vain.*

PSALM 127:1

The gentle voice of the ocean waves lapping on the shore was the musical backdrop to our romantic setting. We watched the deepening colors of the setting sun as we held hands looking out across the ocean. Although the meal had long since been finished, we were reluctant to leave from the quaint, almost deserted outdoor restaurant where we lingered, enjoying a moment of quiet solitude and just being together.

I picked up the card he placed in front of me and began to read. A smile slowly formed as I read the closing words, "Will you marry me?"

"I want to hear you say it," I said with a mischievous grin, looking into the eyes of the man I loved. We were halfway around the world, sitting in a small restaurant in China, but it had taken more than an airplane ride to get us to that special moment.

Kevin and I had met seven years before at church. It was a less than spectacular moment as he brushed off our initial conversation, grabbed his bike helmet, and jumped on his motorcycle to return to his college dorm. *Snob,* I thought to myself, turning and walking back to my group of friends talking close by.

Our paths didn't cross again for a couple of years until again at church we found ourselves attending the same function. We talked for a few minutes, realizing we had several mutual friends. *Strange that our paths haven't crossed again until now,* I thought briefly, but let the thought quickly drop as I excused myself from the conversation.

Snob, Kevin thought, dismissing me from his mind as quickly as I had dismissed him.

Inevitably due to church activities and mutual friends, however, a friendship slowly developed between the two of us. Slowly. It would be another three or four years, as our lives ran along parallel paths, before a relationship finally began to take root. But it appeared that we had waited too long as Kevin had decided to dedicate his life to serving God overseas. The preparation needed for the upcoming move left little time for our new relationship to grow, and it appeared our lives were going in different directions.

A year later as Kevin boarded the plane for his first year overseas, we hugged and promised to write. There was no mention of what the future might hold for our relationship. I loved Kevin and felt he was God's choice for me, but I knew from our conversations that he was still holding the relationship at a distance, uncertain if I would be willing to commit to a life in China. He was completely dedicated to God and this call. As for me, I prayed for the people of China, but I certainly didn't want to go live there. At least not yet. I could only pray and trust God for whatever He had in store as I watched the plane take off and slowly disappear from sight. That is when God began to clean house.

The next five months weren't lonely; they were painful. Not because of Kevin's absence, but because I could sense God's continued work in my life, showing me area after area that needed to be turned over to Him. Just when I thought we had reached the end, He would begin to peel back the layer of yet another area, still in need of repair. *What is with this?* I thought over and over as tears became an almost daily ritual. I had dedicated my life to Christ at an early age. Who would have thought He could find so much junk that needed to be dealt with? And why was it all being done now? But even in the midst of this pruning season, I could sense God's healing hand as He worked to remove, rebuild, and restore areas I didn't even know existed.

When Kevin and I were reunited for a brief visit in China five months later, I was confident not only of my relationship with God but the direction my relationship with Kevin was to take as well. As God had cleaned out the deep recesses of my heart, He had also birthed in me an amazing new hunger. Now I was not only willing to go to China, but truly desired to. I knew that God would continue to work in us throughout our engagement and preparation for marriage, but at least, I hoped, the biggest part of the work had already been done.

Dear God, I give my life over to You, every corner and crevice. Change me and mold me to be the woman of God You want me to be. Fill every empty space with You so that if it is Your plan for me to marry someday, I will not look to the man to meet my needs for wholeness, but I will already be whole in You. Amen.

WOMEN OF THE BIBLE

Mary[2]

*We can make our plans, but the
final outcome is in God's hands.*

PROVERBS 16:1 TLB

Invitations, candles, bridesmaids' dresses, flowers. The
period of engagement is filled with an almost endless list of
things to do before the big day. But if you've always thought of
engagement as just a time to plan the wedding, think again.
Although wedding plans are certainly part of this season, even
more importantly, it is a time for vital communication. By this
point, all of the major issues that confront married couples
should have been talked about and agreed upon as much as possible. Now is the time when any remaining areas of concern
should be discussed. Engagement isn't a time to shove issues
under the rug to deal with after the wedding. The more you can
work out ahead of time, the stronger your foundation will be
upon which to build a lifetime of memories. Engagement is the
final stage in preparation for your new lives together.

We have few biblical examples of this season. The most
detailed is that of Mary and Joseph—a pretty rocky engagement,
to say the least. It was during this season that Joseph learned of
Mary's pregnancy—and *he* wasn't the father! It threatened the
entire relationship. In fact, Joseph had decided to quietly call off

---

[2] See Matthew 1:18–25.

the wedding until God intervened by sending an angel to speak to him in a dream.

After the angel's visit, Joseph still had an active role. He had to choose whether to heed the angel's message or press ahead with his own solution, moved by his turbulent emotions. Few seasons in our lives provide such a recipe for emotional turmoil as engagement. This is due to the stress of almost unending wedding details, added financial pressures, and the fact that marriage is one of the biggest life changes a person will ever make. Thankfully, Joseph was obedient in spite of his pain and misgivings. What if he had followed his emotions to determine his actions rather than the voice of God?

In Joseph's case, God's plan was his marriage to Mary, and God blessed his obedience. But what if an engaged person has serious misgivings? In this case, a broken engagement would be a blessing. While it would no doubt be exceedingly painful, a divorce is certainly more devastating, bringing with it a sense of failure and distrust that can affect every other relationship to come. If God has a plan for your life—and He does—surely He will speak to your heart regarding one of the most important decisions you will ever make, that of choosing a mate.

Dear God, as I enter this time of engagement, I submit my heart and all my plans to You. Thank You for enabling me to hear Your voice. Once I have the assurance that I'm entering Your will for my life, help us to make the most of this season, so we will have a solid foundation upon which to build our marriage. As we undertake planning the wedding, I ask for Your wisdom regarding each detail and decision that has to be made and for Your peace to envelop us to ward off stress. Amen.

LIFE LESSONS

1. Take time to hear God's voice regarding the man you are to marry. This is one of the most important decisions you will ever make.

2. Your emotions should not dictate your actions. The busy schedule and emotional strain of this season is very real, but short-lived when compared to your lifetime together. Decisions should not be based on an emotional state of mind, but by following God's peace in your heart—a peace which comes through prayer, reading His Word, and spending time with Him.

3. Make communication and prayer with your fiancé part of the strong foundation you are building. This should increase as you prepare for your lifetime together and continue throughout your married life.

The Treasures of
Summer

NEWLY WED

Janna Long

OF AVALON

(AS TOLD TO KAREN HARDIN)

Can two walk together, unless they are agreed?

AMOS 3:3 NKJV

Marriage can be the most amazing and safe place in the world. It can also be the loneliest at times. I think every girl grows up with the idea of being "Cinderella" as it relates to marriage. It's a nice fairy tale, but not realistic. I realized that the week after Greg and I returned from our honeymoon when everything that could possibly go wrong did.

It was a difficult and lonely time those first few weeks. We seemed to disagree about everything. Having been single for several years—I was twenty-nine and Greg was thirty-three— we had grown accustomed to doing things our own way and having our own space. It was an immediate challenge just learning to share and make concessions for each other. Surface situations such as decorating our home became major problems as we struggled to overcome our differing opinions.

While I realize that decorating isn't one of the most important issues in the world, when you have an entire home to furnish and realize you will be living with it for such a long time, it can be fairly challenging. I remember one afternoon during this difficult period. I had to get away. It was pouring down rain as I got into my car, and I spent the next several hours driving around crying. "Lord, this is really, really hard. Did I do the right thing?" Marriage was so much more difficult than I had ever imagined.

Returning home, my heart was still in turmoil, but as I walked through the door, Greg came to meet me and took my hand. As we sat down to talk things out, he immediately stepped into his role as the spiritual leader and head of our marriage. He began to pray over our relationship, reminding Satan that our marriage was blessed of the Lord and that it was under His covering. Coming back into a place of agreement, we were able not only to acknowledge Jesus as Lord of our marriage, but to recognize that He had put us together for a purpose.

That's not to say there haven't been other issues over the past couple of years, because there definitely have been. Through our own experience, we have realized that Satan especially targets couples and families to divide from within. If he can divide the home, he can destroy every other area of our lives as well. I'm so thankful that Greg has taken the stand as our spiritual leader, because his doing so has laid a strong foundation on which we have been able to build.

One of the major things we have had to learn is how to disagree with each other. Experts say there is a good and a bad way to argue. We are definitely getting better at doing it the good way—that is learning to discuss the issues at hand and work toward a solution rather than attacking the person. We're also getting better at apologizing quickly and moving on. Ephesians 4:26 says, "'In your anger do not sin': Do not let the sun go down while you are still angry." It's not always easy to do this, but we're trying.

We've even found common ground in furnishing our home, although it has taken compromise on both sides, since I like traditional and Greg prefers contemporary. The end result is that our house is a bit of a hodge-podge, but most of all it is warm and inviting; it's truly a home.

Another thing Greg and I have learned is that although we should be able to depend on one another—and we can—we are not to be dependent on each other. Part of the Cinderella fairy tale is that her prince was everything she needed him to be, but that's just not reality, nor is it fair to the person from whom we are expecting perfection. Only God can fill the spiritual hole in our hearts, and it is wrong to lay that burden on any person, especially a marriage partner. Certainly there are times when I get my feelings hurt or feel disappointed. But during those times,

I have to remind myself that God is the only One who will never let me down and He loves me unconditionally.

After three years of marriage, Greg and I are more in love today than we were the day we married. I know the reason is that we have purposed to put God first in our relationship. God will give His children the very best, if they are willing to leave the decision up to Him. For those who are waiting, I know it's hard, but God's timing is perfect and so is His choice of a mate. I'm so glad I waited. Marriage has been the greatest gift imaginable.

Dear God, marriage is hard work! I thought we had everything worked out before we got married, but now issues are popping up. Help us to be loving and kind to one another as we work through difficulties. Surround us and our home with Your peace, and help us come to quick resolutions. Amen.

JANNA LONG and husband, Greg, are part of the award-winning quartet, Avalon. This past year she released her first solo album, *Janna*. She and her husband make their home in Franklin, Tennessee.

THE SANDBOX

Betsy

Each of you should look not only to your own interests,
but also to the interests of others. Your attitude
should be the same as that of Christ Jesus.

PHILIPPIANS 2:4–5

It was an area we had thoroughly discussed before we married. Having come from two different backgrounds financially and having opposite temperaments, we knew financial matters would be an area we'd need to watch. To put it in simple terms, when Jim and I see money, I think, *How much can I spend?* and Jim thinks, *How much can I save?* Jim's more introverted and conservative mind is always thinking toward the future and the importance of saving. I, on the other hand, can immediately think of 101 ways to use any extra money, figuring it will all come out in the wash, so to speak.

Jim has always been very wise where money is concerned, while it has been a challenging area for me. When we met, Jim already owned a home and had a nice car that was paid for. I, on

48

the other hand, had bitten off more than I could chew and drove a very nice car but was strapped big time because of my car payments. Jim had never paid a dime of interest on a credit card, while I always had a running balance. I always paid my bills on time, but credit card interest was a way of life for me.

In spite of this difference, we felt like we had come to a place of agreement regarding money by the time we married. We agreed we would use credit cards, but I agreed that we would pay them off every month and not pay interest charges. Jim, on the other hand, agreed to loosen up on things that were important to me. I'll never forget when he went to a department store to buy makeup with me while we were dating. When he saw how much one little bottle of foundation cost, I could almost hear him swallow hard, although his demeanor didn't change. The beauty salon was another eye-opening experience for him. My haircuts cost more, and I've gotten a perm every three months for most of my life—a lot more expensive when compared to Jim's barbershop cuts.

So we agreed to meet in the middle, no problem.

What we didn't count on was how tight things would become for us financially. For several reasons, I quit work after we had been married only six months. I was experiencing serious burnout from a very stressful job, and it was affecting my physical health as well as my mental well-being. It was clear I needed to stop, or there would be serious repercussions. But we were still making payments on my beautiful car. The car was the first thing to go, but overnight we went from a fairly comfortable amount of income to Jim being our sole support. That is when the fun and games began.

We've never disagreed on the big things financially. Somehow with those we've always been able to come to a place of agreement. It's been those $3.50 impulse items that have sparked the friction and eaten our lunch. At times we have been like two kids playing in the sandbox, fighting for a toy we both wanted. Jim wanted the money; I wanted the toy. If we had had unlimited income, I doubt these attitudes would have ever surfaced, but then what fun would that have been?

In a way it's actually been a good thing because we have both had to work on character issues and deal with our selfishness. We've either had to work it out or live with strife. The latter is not an option—not if we are going to enjoy being married to one another and have God's blessing.

Today things are much easier financially, and it is rare that we have to discuss the inexpensive point-of-purchase items. Thankfully it's just no big deal now, but what is a big deal is that, because we were both willing to lay selfishness aside and meet in the middle, after fifteen years of marriage we are still best friends—and that's something money can't buy.

Dear God, we really do want to get along. Help us put each other's interests above our own. Help us keep the big picture of our relationship in mind, because nothing is worth getting into strife over and jeopardizing the peace in our home. Help us always come into agreement where finances are concerned. Amen.

IS THE "*D*" WORD IN YOUR MARRIAGE?

Karen Hardin

*Let us not get tired of doing what is right,
for after a while we will reap a harvest of
blessing if we don't get discouraged and give up.*

GALATIANS 6:9 TLB

Marriage is more than a public profession of love; it is a union that takes work, self-sacrifice, and prayer to remain vibrant. It requires a decision to work through the obstacles and differences in life as "iron sharpens iron" (Prov. 27:17) to develop a relationship that can truly be one of heaven on earth. If you have entered into marriage with the thought, *I wonder if we'll make it?* then I encourage you to rethink the foundation of your marriage. As my husband and I have counseled with couples either contemplating marriage or experiencing marital challenges, we have found that those who in moments of anger have spoken thoughts of divorce have already mentally taken their marriages to a precipice of destruction.

"I want a divorce," Chris stated almost emotionlessly as she sat across from me seeking comfort and counsel. Chris and I had been close friends for the three years since my arrival in China. She had been instrumental in helping me learn the difficult Chinese language. In turn I met with her weekly to teach her from the Bible and mentor her.

Now sitting across from me in emotional turmoil, she wanted to hear words of consolation and agreement. I offered her neither.

Prior to their marriage, my husband and I had talked repeatedly with Chris and Paul regarding their relationship. While we could acknowledge that God had brought them together, we cautioned them as to the importance of taking time to build a strong foundation before proceeding into marriage. That included developing their communication and listening skills, getting to know each other better, and in general, simply slowing down. They both agreed this was good advice.

What we didn't learn until later was that they had already applied for a marriage license. In China, once the government license is issued, the couple is legally married, even if the public wedding ceremony hasn't yet taken place. This was the case as Chris came to me that morning already demanding a divorce from her "arrogant" American husband even though the official wedding ceremony was still two weeks away!

Amazingly, this same scenario repeated itself almost identically with four other couples over the next several years as the male American teachers on our team found themselves attracted to beautiful Chinese women. Fortunately in these relationships, all participants were believers, but even this important thread of spiritual unity could not totally compensate for the difficulties due to cultural differences, the language barrier, and the unions being interracial.

According to the U.S. Bureau of Census, of first marriages that end in divorce, many end in the first three to five years. For those that don't, the figures indicate that 40–50 percent will eventually end in divorce.[3] But don't let that discourage you or cause you to give up hope. Your marriage doesn't have to fall prey to those figures. Your ability to work through difficulties to build a strong marriage is a decision that should be determined together even prior to the wedding.

For Paul and Chris, they chose the difficult, yet more rewarding road, to work on their communication and other aspects of their marriage. They did not divorce and today have three beautiful children and a happy home. It hasn't always been easy, but they did it and so can you.

Dear God, just as I made the decision to marry my husband, help me remember to continue making the decision to love him, stand by him, pray for him, and communicate lovingly with him. I pray that the word "divorce" will never enter our conversation or our home and that our marriage will be the piece of heaven on earth that You've designed. Amen.

---

[3] U. S. Census Bureau Web site: www.census.gov (accessed December 2002).

WOMEN OF THE BIBLE

Esther[4]

Let each one of you in particular so love his own wife as himself, and let the wife see that she respects her husband.

EPHESIANS 5:33 NKJV

The small glimpse the Bible reveals of this beautiful young woman is a testimony to her commitment to God and her submission to authority—two important character qualities, the latter severely lacking in many people's lives.

Upon the king's decree requiring all beautiful maidens to join his harem, Esther went from living in exile with her cousin Mordecai one day to living in the king's court the next. Faced with this unexpected upheaval of her life, Esther laid down her own "rights" and immediately submitted not once, but in several ways, to several people.

First, she submitted to the king's command and went to the palace. Then she submitted to the instruction of her uncle Mordecai—who had raised her after her parents' death—as he forbade her to reveal her heritage as a Jew. Finally, she submitted to the instruction of Hegai, who was in charge of the king's harem, a total stranger to her at that point.

Submission isn't a popular subject, especially in America where our individual "rights" are so strongly promoted and protected. Many Christians have erroneously embraced this

[4] See Esther 2.

54

attitude as a license to ignore the biblical mandate of submission to authority. Looking to Esther as an example, what did she lose by laying down her own desires and "rights"? As she submitted, she immediately gained the favor of all who saw her—including the king—and her place in history was secured. Submission brought elevation. It usually does. It is a true sign of maturity.

Marriage requires immediate adjustments in lifestyle for both the man and woman. The carefree days of the single life give way to the committed relationship of marriage, where God instructs women to submit themselves to their husbands. Of course this isn't a license for the husband to lord it over his wife; God has also instructed both the husband and wife to submit to one another out of reverence for Christ (Eph. 5:21). Without this submission of our selfish desires, needs, and rights, we can never gain the favor, blessings, and benefits of the "heaven on earth" marriage that God designed.

Esther learned the lesson of submission early on. When faced with a horrible dilemma, she willingly risked possible death to appear before the king uninvited, instead of ignoring the desperate plight of her people. She had the backbone and com-mitment to willingly sacrifice her own life if need be, laying down her own desires for the good of others. Our submission rarely requires that we risk our lives, but it usually does require the death of our own selfish will.

Dear God, help me to lay down my selfish needs and wants so that I may please You and be a blessing to my husband. Teach us what it means to submit ourselves one to the other out of reverence for Christ. Amen.

LIFE LESSONS

1. Be willing to submit to those in authority over you.

2. Learn what it means for you and your husband to submit to one another.

3. Allow God to replace selfish motivations with loving concern for your mate.

4. Obedience and submission bring God's favor and promotion.

CAREER

Luci Swindoll[5]

Happy are those who find wisdom,
and those who get understanding,
for her income is better than silver,
and her revenue better than gold.
She is more precious than jewels,
and nothing you desire can compare with her.

PROVERBS 3:13–15 NRSV

Ready for a giant risk two years out of college, I moved from Houston to Dallas in 1957. Having a degree in commercial art helped me land a job with Mobil Oil Corporation as a draftsman. I thought I'd be there a couple years, then go back to school, because I loved school and everything that went with it. But as I got more into corporate life, I discovered some advantages that seemed more valuable to me. I found I could make a good living, continually learn new and interesting things, feel secure in a job while pursuing all kinds of other interests outside

---

the office, enjoy an esprit de corps at work, and develop a pro-fessional life—something I had never experienced before.

It wasn't always easy, of course. There were days I wanted to throw in the towel—one that was soaking wet with the tears of disappointment over something that didn't go my way, or hard work without recognition, but I hung in there. Ultimately, it paid off, both emotionally and financially.

One of the greatest lessons I tucked under my belt during this time was this: Things of value cannot be had for nothing. My years at Mobil Oil Corporation were the testing ground for this truth. More often than not, deferring the rewards of today gives us the future we dream of tomorrow. We have to spend in order to get—and time, energy, and money are our only mediums of exchange. Count on it, anticipate it, and accept it. When we get this straight and realize there's no shortcut to having what we want, life gets a bit easier. Not problem free, but definitely easier. We quit thinking that life somehow owes us a living. We work. We pray. We study. We're attentive to details. We put first things first. We risk. We believe God means what He says. Unless we live out of these truths, there really is no tomorrow. Everything becomes one endless, tedious, tiresome "today," and there's no growth or change. In short, wisdom never comes.

I remember asking God for wisdom. It was as though He asked me one day when I was praying, "What do you want most, Luci?" I started thinking about where I had been and some of the choices I'd made that led to dead ends. After turning all this over in my mind, I answered, "Wisdom, Lord." That's what I want most. Please, give me wisdom.

Well, when we ask for that all kinds of things begin to happen. God comes in like a flood, altering our world—changing the things we once valued, restructuring relationships, taking away this desire and adding that one, putting our priorities in a new alignment. God grows us up!

When life began giving me the truth, I often felt loss or uncertainty. At times I was adrift without moorings. I experienced fear and redirection, or no direction. I felt afraid. But I knew God was with me and for me. I often didn't have a clue about His inscrutable ways of handling things (and I still don't), but deep inside there was an abiding assurance that He would keep His Word and, somehow, bring me out on the other side.

Dear God, above all things, give me Your wisdom that I might live life to the full. Give me courage to step out in faith, to love, to give, to laugh, to bless others, to be the child You want me to be. May my life bring glory to You. Amen.

LUCI SWINDOLL is a nationally recognized speaker and author of several books including: *I Married Adventure: Looking at Life Through the Lens of Possibility* and the companion journal, *I Married Adventure: Daring to Live the Life You Dreamed.*

You Don't Want To Eat This Food

Brenda

*She sets about her work vigorously; her arms are strong
for her tasks. She sees that her trading is profitable,
and her lamp does not go out at night. She speaks with
wisdom, and faithful instruction is on her tongue.
She watches over the affairs of her household
and does not eat the bread of idleness.*

PROVERBS 31:17–18,26–27

"I want to own my own restaurant," I would tell my room-
mate as we shared an apartment and dreams of our future.

"You're an amazing and creative cook," she'd tell me, hon-
estly believing I would do it someday. Now twenty years later, I
am fulfilling my dream of working with food. It is not unusual
for me to make fifteen cakes in a day. Many say that the treats I
make look too good to eat, which is probably a good thing. You
see, the food I make is fake.

I didn't start out with my own business; I was very content as a stay–at–home mom with three young children and a hard–working husband. So how did all of this come about?

It started eight years ago while vacationing in North Carolina. As we were out combing the tourist sites, an imitation potpourri pie captured my attention. *Twenty–five dollars!* I thought to myself glancing at the price tag. As I examined the piece I thought, *It's not even that good. I can do better than that.*

So when we got back home, I went to work. With a bag of flour and some salt, I found a recipe for salt dough and began experimenting. I included my first pieces in a garage sale a month later and sold over four hundred dollars worth of product. From that moment on, I was hooked and my company, 'Just Dough It!' was born.

Over the next three months, I participated in sixteen craft shows with my faux food. I was amazed at the incredible success. God began to give me ideas on how to make breads, pies, cakes, etc. One customer asked me to make an entire Thanksgiving dinner of my food to display in a model home. It took some creative maneuvering, but with a tin can and some aluminum foil, I created the shape for the turkey; salted, pep–pered, and parslied it; and voilà, it looked great. I found I could make almost anything.

Once I set up my web site, all sorts of orders began pouring in like the order I received from Paramount Pictures for a wedding cake or the one from Universal

Studios in Japan. The CBS show *Hack* also uses my food for their diner scenes on the show. But the most intriguing order was the call from the United States government. For the war against terror, I was contacted to see if I could create a model of anthrax to use in training our soldiers how to recognize the real thing!

At times it can be difficult juggling the needs of my husband, three children now in their teens, and my home-based business, but its lots of fun. The Bible says that every-thing believers put their hands to will prosper. I believe God has given me the creativity and ability for what I am doing, and He is causing it to succeed.

Dear God, thank You for the gifts You have placed within me. Help me to recognize them and develop them to their highest potential to bring You glory in all that I do. Amen.

For additional information on Brenda's faux food creations and her company, Just Dough It, go to her web site: www.justdoughit.com.

BUSINESS PROPOSALS AND POTTY TRAINING: THE LIFE OF A WORK-FROM-HOME MOM

Karen Hardin

You will eat the fruit of your labor;
blessings and prosperity will be yours.

PSALM 128:2

"Mom, I need to go pee," called my three-year-old daughter, Holly.

We were once again working on potty training for the umpteenth time. Fortunately, this time we were finally seeing results. Whoever said girls train easier than boys?

"Again? Are you sure?" I asked, hoping she would say no so I could work, knowing she wouldn't.

Working at home is a blessing, don't get me wrong, but it carries its own set of frustrations. Potty training, for example.

The pressure of project deadlines mixed with the constant inter-
ruptions of potty training is a challenge unrealized by those in an
office setting. Let's just say it takes patience and organization to
a level of sainthood that I have yet to achieve.

The morning had not gone well. As any work-from-home
mom can tell you, we have to run a pretty tight ship. My morn-
ings go something like this: prayer (if I'm lucky), shower (if I'm
really lucky), kids up and dressed, diapers to change, breakfast,
diapers to change, feed the cat, more diapers to change, and don't
forget homeschool. Only when all areas come under calm
control is there any hope of sitting down at the computer to
work. Throw in any number of variations, and the entire schedule becomes skewed. Sick days are one such variation; potty
training is another. Late nights are a given. Who needs sleep?

I've never been an "all I want to do is get married and raise
my kids" kind of person. While I do believe that being a mom is
one of the highest callings from God, I also know—at least for
me—that I need another outlet to maintain sanity. Extremely goal
oriented, I obtain great satisfaction from completing projects and
marking them off my list.

In my role as Mom, I rarely obtain this satisfaction. One
day blends into another, a blur of activity with
seemingly little results. No matter how many
times a day we pick up toys, there *always*
seem to be more. No matter how many
diapers I change, I know I have only a
short reprieve before the task is required

again. No matter how many times I help wash little hands, it is an exercise in futility to hope that they can remain clean for the rest of the day.

At least once I get to my computer I can see tangible evidence of progress. A letter written, a phone call made. With growing satisfaction I watch as items are slowly crossed off my list. Motherhood isn't nearly so cut and dried.

"Mom!" Holly calls again, now dancing with the pressing need. I push away from the computer and run with her to the bathroom, hoping we can make it in time. We did.

A smile slowly spreads across her face as she successfully completes her mission. "I did it, Mommy!" she declares. Her face flushed with success, she slaps my hand in a high-five and scurries back to her dolls spread across the floor.

I watch her for a moment and then turn to see our youngest, Joshua, now twenty months old, climbing all over his six-year-old brother. They tumble together in play as Joshua "wrestles" his brother who has allowed him to "win" again. Both begin to laugh as papers and toys are scattered in disarray across the just-cleaned floor.

I smile and sigh, returning to my desk and the computer located in the family room, just a few feet away from my three treasures. Yes, they are also my constant disruptions. However, I'm convinced the trade-off of a peaceful and quiet working environment for their presence is worth the extra effort and lost sleep required to work at home. It may not work for everyone, but the relationships and memories we are creating compel me to keep trying after the most frustrating days.

I begin again on the half-finished letter before me when I see my to-do list taped to the computer screen. I pick up my pencil and write down potty training at the bottom of the long list, slowly marking a dark line across the word. It feels good to enjoy the accomplishment of the moment, realizing it may only last until the next potential accident. It is a moment cherished nonetheless.

So it is with our children. Childhood is just a moment in time that will soon be crossed off the list as they progress into a new season of development. It is a moment to be cherished as I wipe the peanut butter off my computer.

Dear God, help me to keep my focus on You. Please show me how to provide my children with the quality time they need, while juggling the demands of work. You are my strength, and I receive Your grace and peace. Amen.

WOMEN OF THE BIBLE

Deborah[6]

May the favor of the Lord our God rest upon us; establish the work of our hands for us—yes, establish the work of our hands.

PSALM 90:17

Deborah was not only a judge of Israel, she was the only judge distinguished as a prophet as well. Knowing her to be a woman of wisdom, the people went to Deborah to settle disputes. In addition, she was anointed to speak the prophetic word of the Lord to the people and leadership of the land. In her career, it is evident that Deborah walked in the gift God had given her. According to Proverbs 18:16 NKJV, "A man's gift makes room for him, and brings him before great men." This was evident in Deborah's life as she spoke with authority, confident of her gift and message, even in the audience of the king.

It is interesting to note that although Deborah was married, she was the one the Lord called to lead Israel and not her husband. Other than this, however, we receive no insight regarding her home life. Did she have children? Were they grown? How did she juggle the responsibility of being a wife with having a career and possibly being a mother?

What we do know is that Deborah was called of God and she was obedient.

---

[6] See Judges 4 and 5.

The ability to balance the demanding roles of wife and mother with a career and/or leadership is not easy, but it can be done. How did Deborah keep her life in balance? Her close relationship with God and the ability to discern His voice were certainly key elements to her success.

Whether your career takes place in an office, on a stage, or at home, God has made His requirements clear: "He has told you what he wants, and this is all it is: to be fair, just, merciful, and to walk humbly with your God" (Micah 6:8 TLB). Like Deborah, you, too, can excel in your career and be a blessing to many.

Dear God, give me Your strength and ability to accomplish that which You have planned for my life. Help me to balance my busy schedule and to keep my priorities in line with Your will. Amen.

LIFE'S LESSONS

1. Are you seeking God's plan for your life, or simply climbing the corporate ladder? A close, personal relationship with God, which will enable you to discern His voice, is the key to true and lasting success.

2. As you acknowledge and develop the gifts God has given you, He will open amazing doors of opportunity.

3. Let God help you prioritize your day to maintain healthy relationships along with a successful career.

MOTHER OF
YOUNG CHILDREN

Denise Jones

OF POINT OF GRACE
(AS TOLD TO KAREN HARDIN)

*All your sons will be taught by the LORD,
and great will be your children's peace.*

ISAIAH 54:13

"*Okay* God, so what am I doing wrong?" I cried out. Tears streamed down my face as I drove away from the summer camp facility where I had just dropped off my two boys, ages two and four, for the day. What was supposed to be a day of fun–filled activities had suddenly turned into an emotional episode of sep-aration anxiety.

Replaying the incident in my mind, I noted the smiling faces of all the other children as they waved cheery good–byes to their parents in comparison to my own wailing children whose cries still echoed in my ears and tugged at my heart. And that is where I made my mistake—comparison. That should be the first commandment to parents: Thou shalt not compare thy children to others.

I don't think it matters whether you are on the road traveling like I am or are a stay-at-home mom or a working-outside-the-home mom. I think we are all tempted to worry about our children. We are all concerned about raising them in the healthiest and most secure environment possible. This has always been a burden for me as I struggle to provide a flourishing home life when we are so often on the road.

As I made my way home that day, there wasn't a particular verse that came to my mind; instead I began to think on the message I had been studying recently in the Gospel of John. Over the past year, I have been working my way slowly through this book of the Bible. It's a simple, yet powerful message. In studying John, I have realized my own need to trust God more. I finally came to the point where I realized I was stressing so much about my ability as a mom and doing the right thing for my kids that I wasn't trusting the Lord. He is the One who has called me to a singing ministry, and He will provide what my children need, even though our lifestyle may be different from that of the average family.

I can't say I have totally conquered this issue yet, but I'm working on it. Jesus is the Bread of Life, and I have found peace in that. I am learning to trust Him to give me that motherly instinct to know what my children need in each situation, to help me love them and teach them according to their different needs and personalities.

One particular verse I have been teaching my boys often comes to my mind: "When I am afraid, I will trust in you" (Ps. 56:3). It's a good word for us mothers as well as for our children. We must trust and depend on God daily. It really goes back to the basics of spending time with Him. His well is deep, and it is always available for us to draw from. It is what will sustain us in the days ahead.

Dear God, You know I want to be a good mother more than anything in the world. It's tough to know how to do the right thing all the time. Give me Your wisdom to know what each of my children need at any given time. If I'm handling something in a way that hurts their little hearts or doesn't bring glory to You, please bring it to my attention. Amen.

DENISE JONES is part of the award–winning group, Point of Grace. In addition to their musical contributions, the group has recently been traveling across the United States, speaking to thousands of teens and young girls. Their conferences, Girls of Grace, inspire those who attend to embrace a lifestyle of purity for Christ. Their newest album, also titled *Girls of Grace*, is available in Christian bookstores.

CHILDREN AREN'T CANS TO BE LABELED

Vikki

*Do not exasperate your children; instead, bring them
up in the training and instruction of the Lord.*

EPHESIANS 6:4

Companies spend millions of dollars on marketing research
in order to create the perfect label for their product. The vibrant
colors and trendy slogans become its recognizable trademark for
years to come. While labeling might be effective in selling a
manufacturer's product, it can destroy the self-esteem of a child.

Unfortunately, it is common for children to receive labels
from family members, teachers, and peers, even though it may
be unintentional. *Hyperactive, stupid, lazy, ADD, ADHD* are frequent designations. Once labeled, the child begins to feel like the
proverbial square peg in a round hole, a mold that can be difficult to break out of. It is little wonder these children suffer from
rejection, low self-esteem, and little self-confidence.

I can speak from experience because I have had to face this challenge with my own three children—ages ten, eight, and five—who have had the words *inattentive* and *disruptive* combined with *dyslexic* and *ADHD* applied to their young lives by certain teachers. At a loss to know how to combat these devastating labels, my own upbringing provided no stable example to follow. Growing up in an abusive home where my parents divorced, I have had to set aside many of the parenting skills I saw modeled in my childhood and replace them with the godly principles of the Bible.

I've had to retrain many of my natural responses, such as the tendency to yell at my children during times of frustration, and discipline myself to use more constructive means of communication instead. Children mirror what they see us do and how they see us respond, and I didn't like the negative reactions that were beginning to emerge in my children. Just as I was becoming aware of my need for change in this area, another obstacle surfaced.

After we relocated to another state due to my husband's employment, we noticed that Ashley, our oldest, was not adjusting well. She had difficulty making friends, and her grades were low. Our attempt to help her with her homework in the evenings was met with frustration. This frustration only escalated once her younger brother, Austin, learned to read and in a short time easily surpassed her level. Schoolwork and good grades came almost effortlessly to Austin. For Ashley, just to make average scores took supreme effort.

"It's not fair, Mom," wailed Ashley one evening as she struggled to complete her assigned homework. "Austin's already finished. I'll never get done." My husband and I watched helplessly as Ashley's self-esteem plummeted. This was perplexing to us because in other areas Ashley proved to be extremely bright. We had no idea what to do or where to go for help.

Finally, Ashley was diagnosed as having dyslexia. While it brought some relief to understand why she was struggling so, it did little to resolve the problem or relieve her frustration. Naturally, Ashley's learning disability created additional stress for the entire family, but I didn't realize the impact it was having until one day I saw Austin sucking on his shirt, a habit that had started a couple of years ago for no apparent reason.

"Why do you suck on your shirt, Austin?" I asked as I pulled it out of his mouth and tried to smooth down the wet and puckered material.

"Because you're always yelling at us," he said quietly. "It makes me nervous."

Ouch! I thought, as the repercussions of my actions became clear. Without realizing it, I had allowed my own frustration and response patterns from my parents to dictate my relationship with my children. Something had to change and fast.

Although my own parents did not provide a godly example of parenting, I knew I didn't have to follow in their footsteps. Instead I have chosen to follow the godly principles taught in the Bible. Instead of tearing us apart, the challenges we have faced have only forced me to reach deeper into the Word of God for help not only for my daughter, but also for our entire family.

It is a great relief to know that just because I came from a dysfunctional family does not mean I have to reproduce that pattern in my present family. It just means we have to seek God for wisdom each day to help us establish a peaceful, loving, and stable home.

Dear God, since You made my children, You know exactly what they need in order to develop properly and overcome the challenges they face. Give me wisdom as I train, teach, and shape them; and fill our home with Your peace to provide the stability they need. Amen.

DON'T ALL MOTHERS WEAR EARPLUGS?

Karen Hardin

> Jesus said, "Come to me, all you who are weary
> and burdened, and I will give you rest. Take my yoke
> upon you and learn from me, for I am gentle and
> humble in heart, and you will find rest for your souls.
> For my yoke is easy and my burden is light."
>
> MATTHEW 11:28–30

"Excuse me," I repeated to our seven–year–old, the oldest of our three children. "Didn't you hear me speaking to your father?"

"But Mom, it's urgent. I have to tell you now," complained Michael, still unwilling to wait for his turn to speak. Conversation etiquette is a lesson we're working on diligently with our children. So far we have deduced that they all really enjoy talking. Unfortunately, there are many times in which all three are speaking to me at the same time. Such a moment usually results in a rising decibel level that seems to rival the loudest of rock concerts.

Our constant reminders to stay quiet until a current conversation is completed have been a difficult premise for their young minds to grasp. Instead, they raise their voices to talk over the communication already in progress. The close confines of a vehicle only magnify our communication woes, which are further complicated when our daughter, who loves to sing, begins belting out another round of "Father Abraham."

Did I mention that as an introvert, I reenergize through times of quiet solitude? Nobody explained in the "Mother-to-Be Handbook" that I would forfeit any resemblance of quiet for at least twenty plus years as the cute "Ma Ma," "Da Da" gradually turns to "Mom, he hit me!" to the inevitable "Mom, it's my turn to use the car!" By six o'clock, as I'm preparing dinner, my husband enters to find his loving children and rather frazzled wife.

"Honey, Holly is asking you a question," he says firmly. "Why aren't you answering?"

My glazed-over eyes should have been a clue, but his comment brings me back to reality and the needs of my children. Yes, I admit that at times I have joined the ranks of those mothers I vowed I would never become. I have developed the resourceful ability to disengage my weary ears and continue my work almost oblivious to the rising noise level. My husband gives me that look that tells me I'm busted and need to remove the mental earplugs, which have brought my short reprieve.

In truth there are days I wish I could "get off work" at five o'clock, take off my "mother" hat with no further demands for the rest of the evening—days my body and brain have little left with which to continue giving to the little ones entrusted to my care. It is in those moments that I am comforted by the fact that I have a Father whose work shift never ends. He is ever waiting to take my hand, provide security and comfort, and let me pour out the frustrations of my heart to Him. Thankfully, God never wears earplugs.

Dear God, it's been a difficult day. I'm tired and need to rest. Please restore my soul and lead me beside still waters. Help me to refuel so I can give to my family once again. Amen.

WOMEN OF THE BIBLE

Rachel[7]

Where envying and strife is, there is confusion and every evil work. But the wisdom that is from above is first pure, then peaceable, gentle, and easy to be intreated, full of mercy and good fruits, without partiality, and without hypocrisy.

JAMES 3:16–17 KJV

Rachel may have won out over her sister Leah for Jacob's heart, but it was Leah who was elevated to the esteemed position of motherhood. At this point, Rachel had been unable to bear children, and she became consumed with jealousy, comparing herself to her sister—obsessed to the exclusion of all else. Eventually she became so irrational that she demanded of Jacob, "Give me children, or I'll die!" (Gen. 30:1).

In her jealousy, Rachel established the unhealthy pattern of making comparisons and showing favoritism, which poisoned the relationships between her children, Joseph and Benjamin, and of their half brothers, Leah's children. From the moment they were born, Jacob openly favored Rachel's children over Leah's, putting their safety, needs, and comfort ahead of those of his other children, in turn setting the stage for Joseph to be sold into slavery at the hands of his jealous brothers.

As mothers we must work to create loving relationships with our children, as well as to help them to have healthy relationships

---

[7] See Genesis, chapters 29 and 30:1–26.

with one another. Each child possesses different gifts and a different personality, and it is our responsibility to seek God as to how we can help develop their strengths. It is up to us to teach our children how to celebrate one another's differences instead of allowing favoritism and jealousy to creep in and eat away at the family foundations. The ability to respect, honor, and share with others is just as important for families with one child as it is for families of many. Ultimately, they are the principles for a successful life.

Dear God, help me to recognize the strengths of each of my children and to never show favoritism. Help me to be fair and consistent in my love and discipline and to instill in them mutual respect. As we celebrate our differences, may we as a family do more than any one of us could do alone. Amen.

LIFE LESSONS

1. Trust God for the wisdom and insight you need each day to be the mother your children need you to be.

2. Work to establish healthy and loving relationships between siblings as well as their peers. Teach your children to celebrate each other's differences and those of their friends.

3. Ask God to help you recognize and understand each child's unique gifts and personality without bestowing favoritism.

HELP! I'M THE MOTHER OF A TEENAGER

Stormie O'Martian[8]

Listen, my son, to your father's instruction and do not forsake your mother's teaching. They will be a garland to grace your head and a chain to adorn your neck.

PROVERBS 1:8–9

It's the best of jobs. It's the most difficult of jobs. It can bring you the greatest joy. It can cause the greatest pain. There is nothing as fulfilling and exhilarating. There's nothing so depleting and exhausting. No area of your life can make you feel more like a success when everything is going well. No area of your life can make you feel more like a failure when things go wrong.

PARENTING!

The word itself can bring contradictory emotions to the surface. We try to do the best we can raising our children.

---

[8] Excerpt reprinted by permission. Stormie O'Martian, *The Power of a Praying Parent* (Eugene, OR: Harvest House Publishers). Copyright © 1995, p. 63.

Then, just when we think we've got the parenting terrain all figured out, we suddenly find ourselves in new territory again as each new age and stage present another set of challenges.

That is where I found myself. The mother of a teenager.

When my son was fourteen years old, he covered his bedroom walls with posters of the musicians he admired most. The problem was that in some of the pictures both the attire and the music being represented were offensive to his father and me and not glorifying to God. When we asked Christopher to take those particular posters down and explained why, he balked, then, with a less than humble spirit did what we asked. A short time later, however, he replaced them with new ones, which were just as bad. We again confronted him, took appropriate disciplinary measures and this time we took them all down for him.

Christopher was not happy, and we recognized we were dealing with the early manifestations of a rebellious spirit. So we decided to do as the Bible says and "Put on the whole armor of God, that you may be able to stand against the wiles of the devil" (Eph. 6:11 NKJV). We prayed, we employed the Word of God, and we professed our faith in God's ability to make us overcomers. We did battle in the Spirit and witnessed the peace of God take control of the situation. Our son's attitude changed, and the next time he put up posters they met the requirements we, as his parents, had established.

Dear God, it is so difficult raising a teenager in this crazy, mixed-up world. Help me to stand strong in prayer to fend off the devil's attempts to make my children rebel and turn away from You. Create within my children hearts that hunger for You, and give them a desire to live godly lives. Help me to be loving, fair, and firm. Amen.

STORMIE O'MARTIAN is the best-selling author of *The Power of a Praying Parent*, *The Power of a Praying Wife*, *Stormie, Just Enough Light for the Step I'm On*, and *Greater Health God's Way*. She and her husband, Michael, have been married for more than thirty years and have three grown children, Christiopher, Amanda, and John David.

TEEN TALK

Debby

> *The righteous man leads a blameless life;*
> *blessed are his children after him.*

PROVERBS 20:7

I have been Mom to three teens, my oldest having just graduated from college, my youngest still in high school. If any one thing has worked for my husband and me, it is that we have stayed very involved with our children as they have grown up. We have made sure that the communication lines have always been open, including for those typically difficult conversations— like that all-important birds-and-bees discussion.

When each of our children turned thirteen, the boys got to take a special trip alone with their dad, and my daughter and I had a special weekend getaway. Stacy and I had a fun trip that included a mother-daughter photo shoot at Glamour Shots on our way out of town to a beautiful old mansion that had been converted to a cozy bed-and-breakfast. After a leisurely breakfast the next morning, we spent the day shopping. These times were a "passage of rights" if you will, marking our children's entrance into the teen years.

These trips provided not only a time to develop special memories, but more importantly they gave us a platform for more open communication. Now older, our children joke about the audio tapes they each "endured" on these trips, which opened discussions about sex, changes in their bodies, and other difficult issues our children face. And though we all laugh now, it provided the needed atmosphere to communicate regarding areas that too often become pitfalls for teens.

Since that time we have worked to maintain these open lines of communication. I knew we had succeeded when our oldest son, Shawn, returned from a missions trip a few years ago. Shortly after his return, we attended a small team get-together in which the group shared pictures and stories to commemorate the trip. As we left that evening, Shawn, with uncharacteristic emotion, turned to us with tears in his eyes as he began to share how much the trip had meant to him and how grateful he was that we let him go. I was thankful for the opportunity of the moment, that the communication lines had remained open and he felt safe to share with us the true thoughts of his heart.

Dear God, as my teens mature, I realize they have close friends with whom they share their daily activities. But I pray that You would help us to keep our communication open and close so that they will always feel safe to share the deep thoughts of their hearts, as well as their hopes and fears about the future. Amen.

THIS CAN'T
BE MY SON

$\mathcal{S}$arah

Even a child is known by his actions,
by whether his conduct is pure and right.

PROVERBS 20:11

If you would have told me ten years ago some of the challenges I would be facing now, I would have laughed. Rebellion, deception, lying? Not my children. After all, we loved God and had raised them in a Christian home with godly values. They were all tender, loving children. We had always prayed over them and tried our best to train them up in the way they should go as instructed in Proverbs 22:6. *So where did we go wrong?*

When my children were younger, people often stopped us in restaurants or stores and told us, "We've been observing your children. They are so polite and well behaved." It warmed my heart as I thanked God for our sweet and obedient children.

We had made the decision to homeschool our children through their elementary years, which created a special bond that was evident even to the casual observer. Of all our children, Aaron, our oldest boy, was probably the most affectionate. He would often come running in from outside with flowers or an impulsive hug and kiss. Parenting was such a joy—that is until things began to change.

I know that one major catalyst in our situation was our decision to enroll our children in a private Christian school after many years of homeschooling. While our daughters were able to make the transition and maintain their loving spirits and Christian values from their upbringing, our oldest son slowly changed before our eyes. Relentlessly, peer pressure chopped away at his self-esteem, creating in its place a young man struggling to find his place.

"You can't make me do anything!" Aaron said defiantly in yet another challenge to our authority.

I shook my head in disbelief. This was my son. I had never had anyone talk to me as he had over the last few months. But as he said the words this time, the reality finally sunk in. *He's right, I can't make him do anything,* I thought in disbelief, blaming myself for his confrontational behavior.

In the midst of these kinds of conflicts, it is easy to get tunnel vision. It sometimes seems as if no end is in sight as self-pity and doubt wipe out each new resolution to have faith. But just when it seems all hope is gone, the once gentle son reemerges, even if briefly, to let us know, yes, he's still there. And once again our hope and faith are restored, and we pray for God's promises regarding our son to be realized.

We're not giving up or giving in to the challenge before us. Had we never experienced this difficult season, we also would never have understood the great need for compassion, mercy, and tough love toward troubled teens. Look around you. Our society is full of young men and women testing the limits as they search for a place to belong. Many even come from Christian homes.

Our job is not to abandon, condemn, or reject these children. Instead, through prayer, love, and godly wisdom, we are to continue reaching out to bring them back. Franklin Graham, Richard Roberts, and even President George W. Bush went through a rocky season of rebellion in their youth. Thankfully, through the prayers and continued efforts of parents and godly mentors, today these individuals are being used for a greater purpose.

While we hope our children can avoid these pitfalls, our job is to remain steadfast during trials like these. For some this may require making difficult decisions to take even firmer steps to curb the rebellion if more common means produce no results. Tough love is an investment in our children's future. Ultimately, we must have faith that God's arm is not too short to draw them back to Himself as we pray on their behalf.

Dear God, grant me the strength, wisdom, and patience needed each day to encourage my teens in the way they should go. When we don't see eye to eye, help us to disagree without being disagreeable. I pray that You will protect their hearts, so they cannot be stolen by the enemy. Amen.

WOMEN OF THE BIBLE

Mary,

*Jesus grew in wisdom and stature,
and in favor with God and men.*

LUKE 2:52

Even in biblical times, parenting during the preteen and teen years must have been difficult. Think of Mary, the mother of Jesus, for example. Although with Jesus she didn't have to deal with rebellion and some of the other problems many parents face, she did face issues that were every bit as serious, when you consider the call on Jesus' life.

The Bible gives us a glimpse into one such example when Jesus was only twelve. He and his family had traveled to Jerusalem, but when the rest of the family was returning home, Jesus remained behind—alone. To make matters worse, He did so without his parents' knowledge or permission. Twelve! Can you imagine the panic when His absence was finally realized! After locating Jesus in the temple, they said to Him, "Son, why have you treated us like this? Your father and I have been anxiously searching for you" (Luke 2:48). It is not difficult for us to imagine Mary and Joseph's anxiety during this episode.

During the season of parenting preteens and teens, we as parents must be willing to expand the boundaries of freedom we

---

[9] See Luke 2:41–50.

allow our children to have, but this freedom is not without guidelines or supervision. Although our growing children begin to look like adults (as some exceed the height of their parents!) and think they are adults, we must remember they are not adults. It is an awesome thing to realize that God has entrusted us with the duty of shaping our teens' lives and character. Allowing them to stretch their wings as they prepare to leave the nest is an essential part of the maturing process, and at no other time is God's wisdom more crucial. Thankfully, He makes this wisdom available when we call on Him for help.

Dear God, I need Your wisdom as I guide my teens through this challenging season in their lives. Each day they face decisions and opportunities of which I have no knowledge or control. Help them make godly decisions. Give them a hunger for You and a desire to follow Your path. Amen.

LIFE LESSONS

1. As your children grow, allow their level of responsibility to grow as well.

2. Develop a listening ear to encourage communication without resorting to an unsolicited lecture.

3. God has entrusted you with the awesome responsibility of helping to shape your teens' lives. He will give you the wisdom, grace, and patience you need to complete the job successfully.

MIDLIFE ADULT, STILL SINGLE

Kathy Troccoli[10]

It is good for me to draw near to God;
I have put my trust in the Lord GOD,
that I may declare all Your works.

PSALM 73:28 NKJV

In Nantucket Island, off the coast of Massachusetts, it was a cloudy, windy day. Cobblestones lined the main street, and small shops and restaurants were attached together with old-fashioned elegance. As I passed them, I knew each had a story to tell. I could almost hear faraway voices from long ago places beckoning. I couldn't help but feel in every sense Nantucket's romantic atmosphere; I felt its embrace, and I longed to share it with someone I loved.

---

[10] Excerpt reprinted by permission. Kathy Troccoli, *My Life Is in Your Hands* (Grand Rapids, MI: Zondervan Publishing House). Copyright ©1997.

While it was a fairy-tale atmosphere, the damp breeze blowing in from the shore was real enough. As I returned to the inn where I was spending the night, I felt that deep, familiar longing. I closed my door and fell to my knees. I thought how much I would love to be strongly but gently held at that moment. Like so many other times, I tearfully expressed my feelings, and God listened. "You alone can fill me with the peace and comfort I need right now. I believe You see the depths of my heart. Every turn, every corner—every cry. You can meet my every need." There was a long silence, then my voice broke through the quiet. "I realize You were right beside me today. You put me in an environment I loved, and my desire to be in love was met in a very unique way. In a way I hadn't expected. You, Jesus, are the man in my life. You've been here all along. You are my beloved. You are the One I have betrothed my life to. You've granted me this day and the sweetness of Your presence."

As I listened to myself pray, I was reminded of my covenant with Him—intimacy with Him. Marriage or not, Jesus will always be my bridegroom. Always be my first love. I realized that we had a memory-making day together and that He had lavishly given me many of the kinds of things I cherish. I truly am in the midst of a love affair that will last for all eternity.

You are His bride. You are His love. What a romantic God we serve. "I belong to my lover, and his desire is for me" (Song of Songs 7:10). Don't ever forget the place you have with Jesus. It is a place that is reserved for you and you alone—so close to His heart that on some days if you close your eyes and listen intently, you may hear His very breath. It is His breath that continually breathes life into your soul. You are so deeply loved. Walk arm in arm with Him today. Your eternal escort. Your faithful bridegroom. He will never let you go.

Dear God, thank You for Your presence. It is so real! Even in my loneliest moments, You are there—to laugh with me, to cry with me, to listen, and to love me. Thank You for being the lover of my soul. Amen.

KATHY TROCCOLI is a singer-songwriter who has garnered four pop radio hits as well as two Grammy nominations and thirteen Dove award nominations. She tours nationally and has appeared on such shows as *The Tonight Show with Jay Leno*, *Live with Regis and Kathie Lee*, and *Entertainment Tonight*.

ARE YOU A "WHOLE," OR DO YOU HAVE A "HOLE"?

Debra

*The peace of God, which transcends all understanding,
will guard your hearts and minds in Christ Jesus.*

PHILIPPIANS 4:7

Just because a person is single doesn't mean something is wrong with him or her. Most people look at me at age forty-one and don't see any physical reason why I shouldn't be married. So next they often begin to look for other reasons, as I watch them mentally flip through the possibilities in their minds.

My goal in life was to get married and have kids. But since that time, my life has gone in a totally different direction than I had planned. Because I travel in ministry to speak and sing, people who meet me for the first time frequently ask, "Did you think you would be single this long?" To answer that question, I would have to say no. I thought I would probably be married in my twenties and have 2.5 kids by now. But that isn't the way it has worked out.

It's not that I haven't had the opportunity to marry, but I don't believe I have had the *right* opportunity. Early on I made a commitment to the Lord that until I have fulfilled all that He has planned for me as a single person, I am willing to wait to have the mate He has chosen for me. I realize that this is a season in my life, and it is a choice I've made.

People can make the decision to be married at thirty, for instance, and by pursuing that decision many do marry by a specified age. Unfortunately, there are also many who are divorced because they made a choice that was not necessarily led by the Spirit of God.

I believe God's plan for marriage is for two "wholes" to come together, meaning we must be complete in Him as single people before we are ready to marry. I am totally in favor of marriage and family. My message is to let God lead you. When you walk out that God-plan, there is little room for frustration as you spend time with Him every day, learning to hear His voice. His directing voice is also His correcting voice. If I'm missing God's plan, He can change my course. The bottom line is that I trust God with my singleness and believe that at the point in time that I am to be married and have children, He will guide and provide.

Dear God, I choose to trust You with my singleness, knowing that You have a time and a season for everything. Help me to be patient and to trust You for Your perfect will and perfect timing in my life. Amen.

DEBRA RAMIREZ is a recording artist, motivational speaker, ordained minister, and single. Her musical abilities played a key role in her winning six Miss America Preliminary titles. She was first runner-up in the Miss Arizona and Miss Oklahoma pageants where she was also the Grand Talent Winner. She earned a degree in business management at Oral Roberts University. For ministry and scheduling information contact: Debra Ramirez Ministries, 8177 S. Harvard #225, Tulsa, OK 74137. Or E-mail: drministries@juno.com.

WHO SAID
IT'S NO FUN
BEING SINGLE?

Jean

*He will be the sure foundation for your times,
a rich store of salvation and wisdom and knowledge;
the fear of the LORD is the key to this treasure.*

ISAIAH 33:6

At age sixty–two, sometimes I think, *I wonder why I have
never married yet.* I say *yet* because my mother had a friend who
got married for the first time at age eighty! When I was
younger, I was very focused on education and my career.
Earning my Ph.D. in Adult and Occupational Education was
one of my goals, and from there I went on to work for two uni-
versities. I could have married on a couple of occasions, but it
seemed like I could never make that commitment. I wasn't a
Christian at that time either. I was focused on having a good
time rather than settling down.

I finally ended up dating a man for about twelve years. We had a lot of fun times together, but I questioned his ability to attain the measure of success I could respect. I knew as far as my own expectations were concerned, my husband would have to be a man I could respect for his achievements. While I cared for this man, I decided it was not love. After I drug my feet in the relationship for several years, he finally got tired of waiting for me and married someone else. After that I was like a little kid whose toy had been taken away. I hadn't wanted to marry him at the time, but once someone else did, I began to question my actions.

In a moment of emotion, I quit my job at the university where I was employed and headed to Aspen, Colorado. I had always dreamed of living there, and that seemed as good a time as any. I cleaned condos in order to pay the rent and skied during the day. I thought I would find another man during this new adventure, and I did. It was Jesus.

I had always attended church and called myself a Christian, but had never really given my life to Christ. One Sunday after I had moved to Aspen, I ran across a schoolhouse with a little sign out front announcing a church service. The music sounded lively, so I decided to go in. I had never been to a service like it before. It was during that service that my life was forever changed.

I may be sixty-two and retired, but that doesn't mean my life is over. I still enjoy skiing as a hobby and doing ministry work.

In fact I will be traveling to Algeria with a prayer team soon, taking in supplies for the needy children of that country.

Growing older doesn't have to carry with it a fear of lack or being alone. God has always provided for my needs, and over the years I have learned to depend upon Him for every need and in every situation I face.

Who knows, someday I might get married yet.

Dear God, You said that You would be my husband and walk with me wherever I go. Yet sometimes I still feel so alone. There are times I long for the joy of shared experiences with a tangible someone. Help me to remember that my self-worth and fulfillment come from You. Amen.

WOMEN OF THE BIBLE

Leah"

Charm is deceptive, and beauty is fleeting; but
a woman who fears the LORD is to be praised.

PROVERBS 31:30

Leah was the not–so–beautiful, older sister. At a time when
other girls were getting married, Leah was still at home. And
that, according to her father, was unacceptable. Leah had become
an embarrassment to her father. His solution was to trick
Jacob—who was hopelessly in love with Leah's beautiful
younger sister, Rachel—into first marrying Leah. Once the
deception was discovered, it was too late, but it did little to
warm Jacob's heart toward his new, unsolicited wife.

Fortunately, we live in a time when staying single no longer
carries the same social stigma as in Leah's day. But it can still be
painful if your desire is to be married.

Even if you'd rather be married, though, your season as a
single can be rich and fulfilling. After all, life doesn't start when
a person gets married. Singleness can be a time for both spiritual growth and the development of rich relationships with
others. Many singles have found it to be an enormous opportunity for time alone with God, so they can grow in their personal
relationship with Him. With no commitment to a husband, there
is also time to devote in volunteer service such as feeding the

---

" See Genesis 29:16–28.

poor, serving at church, and reaching out to neighbors in need. This liberal amount of time is rarely available to the same degree once the single days are past.

Look at this season as an opportunity rather than a catastrophe, and allow God to continue His love affair with you, remembering as Paul said, "I have learned to be content whatever the circumstances. I know what it is to be in need, and I know what it is to have plenty. I have learned the secret of being content in any and every situation" (Phil. 4:11–12).

Dear God, help me to be content in this season of being single and to make the most of the time You have made available to me. When I am lonely, surround me with Your comfort. I want to grow in my relationship with You and make myself available for Your service. I trust You to lead me in Your perfect plan for my life. Amen.

LIFE LESSONS

1. Utilize the additional time you have during this season to help others, pray, and grow in your spiritual walk with God.

2. Do not equate the season of singleness with being a season of rejection. They are not the same.

3. If you have been married and are single again, allow God to heal you of hurts and wounds of the past. He wants to fill your "holes" and make you "whole."

The Comfort of

Autumn

THE EMPTY NEST YEARS

Laura Bush[12]

The house of the righteous stands firm.

PROVERBS 12:7

It's a season many women simultaneously desire, yet dread. The desire to experience aspects of life put on hold during the years of raising children battles with the dread of what life will be like as children leave the shelter of home to begin their own lives. First Lady Laura Bush has faced this very dilemma. During the pressure and hectic schedule of working with her husband in his campaign for the presidency, she was also faced with a major transition as a mother when twins Barbara and Jenna Bush marked their journey into adulthood, leaving home for the first time. This is what Mrs. Bush had to say regarding this new season.

> I'm sad of course; leaving for college is such a passage. But I'm thrilled for them, and they're very excited, though they had a great time in public high school. I remember I felt the same

[12] Excerpt reprinted with permission. Shine Magazine (Nashville, TN: September 1999); www.shinemagazine.com (accessed November 2003).

way: even though I had a great time in high school, I wasn't that sad to leave. You're going off to the next thing—bigger, more exciting. Both of them feel that way about college. For parents, it's such a sad and sweet time because you know it'll never be the same. They won't ever really be home again for any long period of time. At least, you hope they won't, I guess.

Jenna and Barbara mean more to us than anything in the world. We really wanted children; we didn't marry until we were thirty and didn't have them until I was thirty-five, so we felt particularly blessed and lucky to get two babies at once. They're very funny girls, a lot of fun. When they were born, their grandfather was Vice President, and we've made a real effort to give them a normal, private life. We've made that effort the whole time they were here with us.

Both sets of our parents were very interested ... in being the best parents they could possibly be. That's really important for children, and we try to emulate that with our daughters.

Dear God, this is such a bittersweet season of life. Help me to allow my children to leave the nest gracefully and not to try to hold on to them. At the same time, I need You to fill the void that their absence creates. Bless my children as they enter the world, and watch over them. Guide their decisions and keep them safe. Amen.

LAURA WELCH BUSH brings her experienced viewpoints, her love of children, and her interest in education to a broad audience as the wife of the 43rd President of the United States, George W. Bush. Her love of education and reading began in her youngest years and guided her to a career as a Texas public school teacher and librarian after earning her Bachelor of Science degree in education at Southern Methodist University in Dallas, Texas, and later a Master of Library Science degree from the University of Texas. In addition to her national initiative, Ready to Read, Ready to Learn, designed to help America's children learn to read, she has also championed women's health issues, especially breast cancer awareness and assistance for abused and neglected children.

MY NEST ISN'T EMPTY—IT'S JUST CHANGING

Pam

> *Jesus said, "The sheep hear his voice and come
> to him; and he calls his own sheep by name
> and leads them out. He walks ahead of them;
> and they follow him, for they recognize his voice."*

JOHN 10:3–4 TLB

I just want to say I hate the term "empty nest" because I don't believe my nest is empty. We will always have a relationship where we will impart to our children, no matter what their age. Our season may change as they leave home to spread their wings, but they will always be part of our nest.

For years I had heard ladies talk about the dreaded empty nest. How after investing nineteen to twenty years focusing all their energy on raising their children, life seemed to lose all meaning once the children were grown. I looked ahead toward my own future. I certainly didn't want to share their experience, so my husband and I made up our minds that we weren't going to experience that syndrome.

Over the next few years after making that decision, Jim and I prayed regarding that very issue as the time neared for our oldest child, Drew, to head to college. He had a dream to play college baseball. Since he was a talented athlete, it looked like his dream would be fulfilled when he received a baseball scholarship from a Christian-based university in Kansas. My husband and I had hoped he would enroll in Oral Roberts University in our city, Tulsa, but as graduation neared, Drew told us emphatically, "I will never go to ORU!"

Disappointed with Drew's decision, we continued to pray over his future until the day for his departure was near. As we prepared to move our son to the Kansas campus, Jim was praying one morning, and the Lord spoke to his heart, *Keep Drew here.*

"It's a little late notice, don't You think, God?" Jim prayed. "I can't burst Drew's dream to play ball. You're going to have to reveal this to him."

We continued to pray over this situation and put it into God's hands. The day finally arrived for the big move and Jim helped our son pack his belongings into the car and they headed out. As they walked onto the university campus in Kansas to move Drew into the dormitory, Drew slowly turned to Jim and said, "Dad, I'm not supposed to be here. I want to go back to Tulsa."

"Where are you supposed to be, and why are you just now telling me this?" Jim questioned gently, knowing full well what the Lord had already spoken to his own heart.

"I'm supposed to be at ORU," Drew finally admitted. "I just couldn't bring myself to say it until now. My stomach hurts, and my heart hurts, and I can't sleep knowing I am about to make the wrong decision," he concluded.

"Now you know what it means to wrestle with God," Jim explained as they turned around to come back home.

As they drove back, Jim shared with Drew what the Lord had already spoken to him a few days earlier. "Why didn't you tell me that before we drove all the way to Kansas?" Drew questioned.

"Because you needed to hear this from God for yourself," Jim wisely instructed.

Now four years later, Drew has graduated from ORU and is on the path God has chosen for him, stronger in his relation-ship with God not only for having heard God's voice for himself, but also for obeying it.

As our children have grown, we, like all parents, have been concerned with how to equip them so they will succeed in life. As Christians, we believe real success means that they will remain true to their relationship with God and follow His path for their lives. The Bible says, "Train up a child in the way he should go, and when he is old he will not depart from it" (Prov. 22:6 NKJV). Yet, we have all met children raised in Christian homes, some even pastor's children, who have totally departed from the Christian faith in later years. So how can that be? As I wrestled with this question as it pertained to my family, the Lord showed me that as we train our children to hear God's voice, they will never depart from it.

We train our children by example. For Jim and me it has been a lifestyle of hearing God's voice and then obeying His direction. Our children have watched us live this way their entire lives, and we have seen God's blessing over our family because of our obedience to His direction. When we spend our time not just raising our children, but training them to hear God's voice, then the next step is for us to trust God and release them to Him.

Dear God, as I watch my children create their own lives and homes, help me to trust You when they make decisions that are not what I would have chosen. I pray that our relationships will remain close and communication clear. I entrust them to Your care, to guard, guide, and protect them. Amen.

CUTTING THE APRON STRINGS

Janet

The LORD is my rock and my fortress and my deliverer;
my God, my strength, in whom I will trust; my shield
and the horn of my salvation, my stronghold.

PSALM 18:2 NKJV

Satia, our oldest child, was entering her senior year in high school when the reality of the impending season began to weigh on my heart. In another year, she would leave for college, out from under our constant supervision. My husband and I had tried to prepare for this season. We had prayed and planned over the preceding years in an attempt to adjust for the inevitable release that must occur. It is scriptural to let go of your children, but that doesn't mean it is easy.

As I watched my daughter approach adulthood, I knew I faced a challenge that had to be resolved. Remembering the worn Christmas apron I had received from my grandmother years before, I went to the drawer and pulled it out. Frayed and yellowed with stains, it was no longer one that I wore, although it maintained sentimental value. I took a pair of scissors and snipped off the two back ties. I then pinned them to the kitchen curtains in front of the sink as a reminder to pray for the impending separation—the cutting of the apron strings—with our own children.

Each day as I washed dishes, I looked at those apron strings and prayed for the wisdom and strength to walk into this next season. I prayed not only for the decisions they would be making, but for the ability to gracefully accept their decisions as the adults they had become. Graduation came and went, and the time of the inevitable separation was drawing close. One evening as my husband, Galen, and I were preparing for bed, I expressed my concern that Satia was not yet home.

He replied wisely, "Honey, it's 10:00 P.M. In another month, you aren't going to know where she is at this time either. You are going to have to learn to trust God."

Dr. James Dobson has said, "You've given them roots, and now it is time to give them wings." It is a trust issue that all mothers must learn.

All three of our children are now married with lives of their own. Although still parents, we have stepped into a different role as interces- sors and counselors when called upon for wisdom. Although it has been difficult, there are many times I have had to learn to simply be quiet and pray. While we never sever the heart-strings, we do have to learn to sever control.

Now when we get together with our children, we look forward to our time with them, but we don't experience a painful sorrow when they leave. God has enabled us to embrace this new season, teaching us to entrust our children to His care.

Dear God, I know I need to cut the apron strings, but it feels like I'm cutting my heartstrings. Give me the grace to walk wisely during this season of life with my grown children. Heal the tender parts of my heart that hurt, and help me to be a great blessing to them. Amen.

WOMEN OF THE BIBLE

Bathsheba[13]

Her children arise and call her blessed.

PROVERBS 31:28

No matter how old your "child" becomes, the parental instinct remains, especially in mothers. As our children near adulthood, it is a new season of increased listening and stepping back, allowing them to take the reigns of their destiny. At that point our role transitions from specific hands−on guidance to a new place of listening and prayer. Advice, while readily avail−able, is not always necessary or appreciated no matter how helpful the intent. The secret is learning when to give it and when to step in and assist if the situation merits. The latter will vary with the growth and maturity of each child. There is a fine line between mothering and smothering, and it is the wise mother who recognizes and heeds healthy boundaries.

While Bathsheba's young adult years were shaded by the sin of her affair with King David, over time she matured into a godly queen—one who learned when to listen, when to speak, and when to fight for the rights of her children. She was so loved by her husband that he distinguished her above the rest of his wives. King David bestowed on her the honor of allowing their child, Solomon, to be the successor to the throne, instead of his firstborn by another wife.

---

[13] See 1 Kings 1:11−52 and Proverbs 31:10−31.

Even when Solomon was grown, Bathsheba continued to pray, wait, and watch. After learning from the prophet Nathan of the impending attempt by the king's son Adonijah to take over the kingdom, she immediately moved into action. Her willingness to heed the wise advice of the prophet and act promptly saved not only her life and Solomon's, but the life of the kingdom itself.

Solomon held his mother in high esteem as she filled her role with grace. His tribute to her is one of the best-loved passages of the Bible, that of the virtuous woman in Proverbs 31.

Dear God, my desire is to be the virtuous woman and mother described in Your Word. Help me know when to listen, when to speak, and when to simply pray as I entrust my grown children into Your hands. Amen.

LIFE LESSONS

1. Whether they will admit it or not, your grown children may still need a helping hand and parental insight. Be available.

2. As your children test the waters of life on their own, they may on occasion fall in. Give them the chance to swim to shore before jumping in to rescue them.

3. Develop a listening ear toward your children to encourage their communication with you; develop a listening ear toward God to know when to pray and when to act.

GRANDPARENTING

Florence Littauer

(AS TOLD TO KAREN HARDIN)

The good leave an inheritance to their children's children.

PROVERBS 13:22 NRSV

My greatest challenge as a grandparent has been lack of time. My mother and grandmother were amazing women. They didn't work outside the home, but spent their days aproned in the kitchen baking delicious-smelling bread, canning string beans, and taking care of their homes. That is the wonderful heritage my own children experienced from their grandmother. But a generation later, many women like me have found them-selves fitting into a new era of grandmothering. We are working women who shatter the fairy-tale image from the past.

Speaking, writing, and traveling in the ministry have kept me from being around my grandchildren as much as I would have liked. And although I have not been in the kitchen cooking deli-cious treats all the time, as did my mother, I have chosen to focus on the major events in the lives of each grandchild. Birthdays, Christmas, music recitals, ball games, and graduations are all significant moments. They are opportunities to say, "Well done! Great job! Wasn't it worth the effort?"

I have been blessed with three exemplary grandsons, now grown, and just recently a new granddaughter not yet a year old. They have brought tremendous joy to the lives of my husband and me. When my husband passed away just recently, two of my grandsons participated musically at the funeral, one even sharing a touching eulogy. They were tender moments in the midst of sorrow. I have never been so proud as I was then of these fine young men who are able to communicate clearly and make a difference in the world around them.

When my grandchildren were born, I wrote each of them a letter detailing the depth of their grandfather's and my joy at their arrival into our world. I also had my picture taken with each of them to commemorate the moment. As they have grown, I have created a scrapbook for each one, and I have included these items in the books along with reflections about the important events and achievements in their lives. At significant moments, I have given them these special books as a memorial of our relationship.

As a grandmother, the most special moments, as far as I'm concerned, are when we are able to sit down one-on-one and talk. These are treasured memories of times in which they open their hearts and give voice to their hopes, dreams, and concerns. I think all mothers and grandmothers desire to instill positive values into their children and grandchildren, and it is through interaction and relationship that we accomplish this.

Being a grandmother has been a rewarding season in my life, and I'm thankful I have had the opportunity to experience it.

Dear God, it's fun being a grandmother! Thank You for giving me that privilege. Help me pour godly wisdom into my grandchildren and to make special memories with them, even when we live far apart. Give me creative ideas of ways to show them my love. I pray that each of my grandchildren will grow up knowing You, serving You, and fulfilling Your plans for their life. Amen.

FLORENCE LITTAURER is a nationally recognized speaker and author of numerous books including: *Silver Boxes, How to Get Along with Difficult People,* and *Personality Plus!* She makes her home in the Palm Springs area.

THE PRAYING
GRANDPARENT

Belinda

The prayer of the righteous is powerful and effective.

JAMES 5:16 NRSV

"I love my daddy, but do I have to go?" Amanda pleaded as the time neared for her bi-weekend visit to see her father. It broke my heart. She didn't want to go and I certainly didn't want to send her, but I had no choice. I had already learned that in the eyes of the court, a grandparent and sometimes even a parent has little rights regarding parental custody cases. I found myself in the unenviable yet increasingly common position of a grandparent fighting for the well-being and safety of her grand-children—in my case after my daughter's divorce.

My daughter, Stacy, married a young man whom she met at school. Although Keith would not have been my first choice for my daughter, when he was attending church he was a wonderful person. However, several years after their marriage, he became involved in a local religious cult. After that things began to go sour. In a short time he became both physically and verbally abusive to my daughter. With nowhere to turn, Stacy and the children moved into our home until she and Keith finally divorced a year and a half later. Unfortunately, this sad scenario is not uncommon with increasing numbers of grandparents now finding themselves raising or assisting in raising their grand-children in less-than-perfect conditions. But that was just the beginning of our problems.

Keith received partial custody of their two young children despite a past history of alcohol and drug abuse. The children's exposure to adult material on television and videos has also been a great concern, but in spite of our efforts to reverse the court's decision, we have been unsuccessful. "God, protect their eyes from what they might see, their ears from what they might hear, and their hearts from harm," I pray each time the weekend visit draws near. I choose to trust God to protect these children when I cannot. We pray and believe His Word that states that there is nothing hidden that will not be revealed and trust that He is able to bring to public light any dangerous situations that may exist (1 Cor. 4:5).

It hasn't been easy knowing the circumstances into which we are sending the children. It terrified us until God reminded us that He is in control. As a grandparent, I realize that my prayers have power to protect these precious children as I commit to pray over them. Legally I may have few rights in regards to their welfare, but spiritually, as a grandparent, I can surround them with my love, faith, and prayers. God has entrusted us as grandparents with a great responsibility to pray for the protection and future of our grandkids. When we are faithful to pray, God is faithful to perform His Word.

Dear God, thank You for the privilege of praying for my children and grandchildren. You said that the prayers of the righteous avail much. Hear my prayer, O God, to protect and deliver my grandchildren from harm and guide them in the way everlasting. Amen.

THAT'S WHY THEY CALL THEM GRANDCHILDREN

Lynn

Children's children are a crown to the aged.

PROVERBS 17:6

Someone once asked me if I believed in love at first sight. I had to think about it a moment before replying and then told them, "Only if it's your children and grandchildren!"

Grandchildren are awesome. That is why they call them grand! But I can tell you that having four grandsons has been totally different than raising my daughters. Did you know that little boys have built-in sound effects? Car and truck sounds never came out of my daughters. I've also learned that as boys get older, their stomachs motorize their legs. I don't care how recently they may have eaten before they come to visit, the first thing they do after greeting us is head to our refrigerator to look for a treat!

I've learned another important thing in grandparenting, and that is to carefully choose the words I speak. One day I was taking my oldest grandson, Brooks, to a doctor's appointment. As is typical at that pediatrician's office, upon arriving I found the parking lot full. Circling around looking for a spot, I muttered to myself, "I'm believing God for a parking spot with my name on it." Sure enough, a few moments later a car pulled out, and we drove in to occupy the vacated space. As I got out and began walking toward the building, I noticed Brooks wasn't with me. Turning around I saw him on his hands and knees looking under the car with a perplexed look on his face.

"What are you doing, Brooks?" I asked.

"I'm looking for your name on the parking space," he said with complete sincerity.

Although an amusing story, it drives home the message that as grandparents we have an awesome opportunity to help mold the lives of our grandchildren through our words and actions. Children take our words literally, often unable to discern between truth and jesting. If we want to instill truth into our grandchildren, it is important that we provide them with the best example possible in both our own actions and communication.

Dear God, thank You for the privilege of being able to help shape the lives of my grandchildren. May my words and actions set a godly example that they can follow. Help me put a watch over my lips and a guard over my mouth that the words I speak will always point them to You. Amen.

WOMEN OF THE BIBLE

Lois

*I have been reminded of your sincere faith, which first
lived in your grandmother Lois and in your mother
Eunice and, I am persuaded, now lives in you also.*

2 TIMOTHY 1:5

Whether still living or not, grandparents play a pivotal role
in our lives. They raised your parents, which in turn influenced
how you were raised.

The Bible notes two very different grandmothers and their
effect on their grandchildren. The first is Athaliah, the mother of
the wicked King Ahaziah. We read in 2 Kings 11:1–12 that when
she learned of the death of her son, the king, she immediately
proceeded to destroy the rest of the royal family so that she
could rule the land in his place. This grandmother was so
obsessed with her lust for power that she killed all of her
grandchildren to obtain her evil goal! All, that is, except one—
Joash—who was miraculously hidden until the priest could
maneuver troops to dethrone the wicked queen.

Contrast that with Timothy's grandmother, Lois. As Paul
wrote to Timothy (2 Tim. 1:3–5), he reminisced about Timothy's
rich, godly heritage passed down from his grandmother to his
mother and finally to him. His heritage was that of sincere faith.

Hebrews 11:6 NKJV says, "Without faith it is impossible to please Him, for he who comes to God must believe that He is, and that He is a rewarder of those who diligently seek Him."

You have the opportunity to leave a godly heritage to your grandchildren by your decisions and actions today. What will you be remembered for? What will be your legacy? The wealth of the world is fleeting, but integrity, character, and sincere faith in God are priceless treasures that will influence your grand-children for eternity.

Dear God, let the heritage I leave for my grandchildren be one of godli-ness, wisdom, and faith. Let my life be an example that will always point them to You, even after I am gone. Amen.

LIFE LESSONS

1. Your actions and decisions today will leave a legacy that will influence your family for years to come. Make them count.

2. The fervent prayers of righteous grandparents for their grandchildren are powerful and avail much. Those prayers keep working even after the grandparents are gone.

3. The patriarchs of the Old Testament spoke blessings over their children and grandchildren that quite literally changed their lives. Follow their example. When you speak God's Word over your grandchildren, He promises that His Word will not return void, but it will accomplish the purpose for which He sent it.

THE SENIOR YEARS

$\mathscr{B}$everly $\mathscr{L}$aHaye

(AS TOLD TO KAREN HARDIN)

Do not be anxious about anything, but in everything,
by prayer and petition, with thanksgiving, present
your requests to God. And the peace of God,
which transcends all understanding, will guard
your hearts and your minds in Christ Jesus.

PHILIPPIANS 4:6–7

Many people ask me, "How does it feel to be a senior citizen?" That's hard to answer, as I am busier than ever. I think many people erroneously associate the term *"senior"* with time to slow down or stop. Nothing could be further from the truth. It is an exciting time of renewed interests and dreams that can now be dusted off after being shelved due to the pressing demands of earlier years.

Whether you are raising children, serving your church or community, whatever your focus, we all live in a fast-paced world. That is why every morning before my husband and I answer the phone, read the paper, or get involved in any of the other areas that are stress points, we take time to sit down and "let the peace of Christ rule in [our] hearts" (Col. 3:15). We take time each morning to read the promises God has given.

Life is filled with potential stress. I know for my husband, Tim, and me, we are constantly pulled in many different directions. I know this is the case for many others as well. As I travel, I repeatedly hear many seniors say to me, "My life is going faster and faster; isn't it supposed to slow down now?" Well, it doesn't necessarily work that way. At a time when Tim and I are approaching the "age of retirement," we have no intention of retiring, for we will always be doing the work of the ministry. What we need is God's peace and calmness in the midst of our activities each day.

Everyone needs peace and serenity, but I think this is especially true for seniors. During this season, many may face the challenges of a more limited income, possible health issues, etc. We need that assurance and peace that God is in control.

When we let stress control us, we're not letting Christ rule and reign in our hearts. Our minds are the key. If we are running helter skelter and every which way all the time, we will be caught up in that kind of lifestyle. However, we can take control of our thoughts and minds. I have found that He cares about every moment of our day.

At this period in our lives, most of us seniors are at a place in which we have a relative amount of control over our time and schedules each day. We need to make sure we put God first in all we do. When we take that step and put the rest of our priorities in order, then we will see His peace fill our lives.

Remember, the Lord wants us to reap all of His benefits. A peaceful heart is one of them.

Dear God, may the peace of Christ rule in my heart. Although there are many reasons I could become anxious, I choose to cast my cares on You because You care for me. Help me to make the most of my days so that my last days will be even more fruitful than my former ones. Amen.

BEVERLY LAHAYE is the founder and chairman of the national organization, Concerned Women for America. She is the author of several books including: *The Spirit-Controlled Woman* and the four-book series, *Seasons of Blessings*. She and her husband, Tim, make their home in southern California.

RETIREMENT DOESN'T MEAN HIBERNATION

Eula Mae

*Teach the older women to be reverent in the way they live,
not to be slanderers or addicted to much wine, but to teach
what is good. Then they can train the younger women to
love their husbands and children, to be self-controlled and
pure, to be busy at home, to be kind, and to be subject to
their husbands, so that no one will malign the word of God.*

TITUS 2:3–5

When I retired from my position with an oil firm, I
thought I would finally have the chance to get caught up on
some reading and working in my garden. But, my retirement
was short lived.

I had been off only a brief time when I began to realize God
might have something more for me to do. I was at church one
day on a short errand when I began to look around me. The
church had been growing quickly, and there were so many

things that needed to be done and so few people willing to volunteer. Now retired, I had some extra time and decided to give a few hours each week answering phones, helping with the Bible school registration, doing extra paperwork, or completing whatever needed to be done. I just made myself available.

I wasn't looking for a new job, but a new job found me. As I continued to offer my time and services to the church, the pastor began asking me to help out on special projects. Since I was just a volunteer, I didn't have a formal office. They set up a small table in the corner of one of the secretary's offices for me to use. Then one day I began to overhear conversations around the office that the pastor's secretary would be changing positions. I immediately wondered how this change would affect me since my small workspace was in her office. I finally asked the secretary, "Do you think the new secretary will mind if I continue to work in here?" I remember how she laughed at my question.

"Eula Mae, *you* are the new secretary. Didn't you know?" she responded.

I was so surprised. The pastor had discussed with me the need to continue working on several projects he had given me and that the church board had approved hiring me part-time, but I hadn't realized that had meant I would be his new secretary! And I was in that position for the next fourteen years, until finally it was time to retire—again.

Retirement doesn't mean it's time to hibernate. Even now I continue to assist at the church as a volunteer in the senior adult ministry, coordinating activities and ministry opportunities for my age group. It's so important to stay around people. If you are in the position that you can no longer drive, don't sit at home and feel sorry for yourself. Ask someone to take you. There's always a way to get to where people are, and you might just discover that God still has something more for you to do.

Dear God, thank You for helping me to use my time wisely. Time is a gift from You—a gift that can never be reclaimed once it is spent. I pray You will continue to guide me in the path and projects You have for me so that I will be productive even in my years of retirement and rest. Amen.

My Provider

Anne

*My God will meet all your needs according
to his glorious riches in Christ Jesus.*

PHILIPPIANS 4:19

I have often had to remind myself that God is my husband.
Alone since my husband walked out on our family more than
thirty years ago after becoming entangled in the deceptive web of
the occult, God has continually provided for me in amazing ways.

One of the greatest miracles throughout the years has been
God's miraculous financial provision for me. As I look back,
one of the most amazing miracles was how a $15,000 trust fund
for my children was miraculously stretched to provide them
both with higher education after graduating from high school.
Each and every need was met over the years as God provided
our manna, our daily needs, just as He did for the Israelites in
the desert long ago. We had what we needed just when we

needed it, but we didn't have a lot of extra. This meant my desire to pursue my artistic interest had to be put on hold.

I have always loved to paint and from time to time would begin to pursue this interest, but just as I would begin to improve, it seemed some crisis would arise, and once again I would have to put this desire on hold. But I have learned that God cares not only about our needs, but also the desires of our heart. He eventually opened the door for me to paint once again.

A few years ago after becoming involved with our local art league, a woman came to speak to our group. She informed us that the community college in our area allowed seniors, sixty years and older, to take classes for free! It was just the opportunity I needed, and I immediately enrolled. For the last three years now, I have received instruction in both watercolor and oil painting. It has been such a delight to finally get to pursue this long-held interest.

Through art I have received the added benefit of making several new friends.

Artists can be such unique and interesting people and from my experience some can be very liberal in their beliefs. Traditional Christian values, which I had often taken for granted, have not been among the belief system of most of my class-mates. Becoming more involved in these college courses, I have had the opportunity to meet people from all walks of life and a variety of backgrounds. Most would never step foot in a church, but God has provided in yet another way by opening the door for me to be a Christian example and mentor in the lives of my classmates as we have become friends. Although I attend a state-run University that does not provide Christian ministries, I have had numerous opportunities to minister to my classmates as I share from my own experience and God's miraculous provision for both my needs and the deep desires of my heart.

Dear God, Thank You for Your continual provision in my life. I know that I can always come to You for wisdom and comfort. You are a faithful and reliable husband to me even when my earthly husband was not. I love You. Amen.

WOMEN OF THE BIBLE
Sarah[14]

Our mouths were filled with laughter,
our tongues with songs of joy.

PSALM 126:2

Sarah laughed at God, but God brought Sarah the gift of laughter.

God promised Abraham that he and Sarah would have a son, even though they were well past their childbearing years. Sarah, convinced in her mind that her body was as good as dead and her day of usefulness past, decided to help God out. Perhaps using her maid, Hagar, she could move things along—a step she would later regret.

When God spoke to Abraham of His plan to give them a child, Sarah laughed in disbelief. Impossible. With that mentality, definitely. Without God's grace, absolutely. But with God nothing is impossible.

Thank God for His grace, even when we lose sight of the promise. When we focus so intently on the natural circumstances—what we can see, touch, or feel—we forget that His work is supernatural.

God honored His word to Abraham, and Sarah did indeed bear a son—Isaac, whose name means "laughter." Sarah concluded in Genesis 21:6, "God has brought me laughter, and everyone who hears about this will laugh with me." God's miraculous gift of Isaac to Abraham and Sarah was the beginning of the fulfillment of His covenant to them. It is an ongoing

[14] See Genesis 15:1–5, 16, 17:15–19, 18:9–15, 21:1–8.

testimony to the fact that He is committed to fulfill His plan for your life as well—regardless of your age or how long it takes.

Has God spoken a dream to your heart that so far has gone unfulfilled? Have you allowed yourself, as Sarah did, to believe your day is over? If so, take heart.

Jeremiah 29:11–13 says, "'I know the plans I have for you,' declares the LORD, 'plans to prosper you and not to harm you, plans to give you hope and a future. Then you will call upon me and come and pray to me, and I will listen to you. You will seek me and find me when you seek me with all your heart.'"

God wants to give you the gift of laughter today as you embrace His promise to fulfill His plan for your life.

Dear God, I've grown weary and discouraged that the dreams of my heart have not come to pass. But I believe these dreams are from You. Restore joy and laughter to my life. Help me to keep my eyes on You instead of my circumstances, for I know that You are greater than any situation I face and You will fulfill Your plans for me. Amen.

LIFE'S LESSON

1. Neither our value nor our usefulness to God are limited by our age. God always has a plan for you.

2. If you have an unfulfilled dream in your heart, don't give up. With God nothing is impossible.

3. Now is a good time to reevaluate this season in your life. God wants to play an active role in your senior years. If you will seek Him, you will find Him when you search for Him with all your heart.

WIDOWED

Lisa Beamer[15]

WIDOW OF 9/11 HERO, TODD BEAMER

Do not fear, for I am with you; do not be dismayed,
for I am your God. I will strengthen you and help you;
I will uphold you with my righteous right hand.

ISAIAH 41:10

"Mrs. Beamer, my name is Nick Leonard from United Airlines. I'm sorry to inform you that your husband was a passenger aboard Flight 93 that has crashed in Pennsylvania."

"I know," I replied calmly. I didn't break down crying hysterically. I didn't yell or scream or make any outburst at all. The United representative sounded almost surprised that I was so calm. I didn't fully realize it then, but God was already giving me an incredible sense of peace.

---

[15] Excerpt reprinted with permission. Lisa Beamer, *Let's Roll! Ordinary People, Extraordinary Courage* (Carol Stream, IL: Tyndale House Publishers) copyright © 2002, pp. 11, 163, 165–166, 307–311.

As I sat on the bed that Tuesday morning, September 11, my world had suddenly come to a halt. For a long time after I saw the crash site on TV and heard the news that it was a United flight that had crashed in Pennsylvania, I stared blankly at the field outside our window, trying to make sense of it all. Just a few short hours earlier, Todd had been lying beside me. Now I was certain he was dead. My day had started out so ... ordinary— with a shower, breakfast, laundry. And then the phone call had come. My mind somehow couldn't reconcile the two realities.

In that dark moment, my soul cried out to God, and He began to give me a sense of peace and a confidence that the children and I were going to be okay. But even that comfort didn't take away the wrenching pain or the awful sense of loss I felt. Nor did it answer the question that continually tugged at my heart. *How can I live without Todd?*

On September 11 Todd Beamer completed his time on earth. His life ended while "daring greatly." He did not die with the "cold and timid souls who know neither victory nor defeat." He has even been called a hero for fighting back against evil, for putting his own life on the line in an attempt to save others.

While his final actions did require great courage, something else he did that morning required even more. In the face of the worst circumstances he could humanly imagine, Todd chose to rest in the words of the Lord's Prayer: "Thy will be done." He put himself in the hands of God, knowing that ultimately that was the only safe place to be. Of course Todd wanted to come home on September 11, but he knew if that didn't happen, God was still in control and would take care of him and of us.

I know I can't change the tragedy of September 11 or even those who caused it, ultimately; I can be responsible only for my own choices. The Bible says that God causes all things to work together for good—not that everything is good, but He will work it for good—to those who love God. Todd didn't claim to be perfect, and neither do I, but we do fall into the category of those who love God. That means as we choose to trust God and follow His desire for our lives, He promises to work everything for good to us both now and in the future.

Although I never could have imagined the awful circum-stances brought about in the life of my family by the events of September 11, I know that promise from God proved true for Todd on that day. That promise proves true for me, too, as I go on from September 11. God has provided so many things: love beyond measure from family, friends, and strangers; the encouragement of knowing people whose lives have been changed because of Todd's example; glimpses of God's per-spective on my life and on our world; and an unexplainable peace in my soul.

My life since September 11 includes many human sorrows and challenges, and every day I must choose how to confront them. I can sink into depression or anger or anxiety, or I can trust that God is working everything for my good. I have chosen to believe God—to believe He loves me and has a plan for now and for eternity. I don't claim to understand, but I choose daily—even moment by moment—to have faith not in what is seen but in what is unseen. The road ahead is uncertain and even scary at times, but I believe that God will provide what's best for me, just when I need it. Even now, in the midst of great sorrow, there is much to be thankful for—a great family, wonderful friends, and a strong community of faith. I try to appreciate my blessings every day.

Of course the three sweetest gifts are often gathered on my lap. To them, "Let's roll!" is not a slogan, a book, or a song; it's a lifestyle. A lifestyle Todd and I began together, and one my children and I will carry on.

Dear God, there are so many unexplainable things that happen in this world, but I believe Your promise to work everything out for my good. Fill me with Your peace, Your strength, Your love; and use me to bring encouragement and hope to others. Amen.

LISA BEAMER and her two sons and infant daughter reside in New Jersey.

CONQUERING THE SPIRIT OF GRIEF

Earline

Do not grieve, for the joy of the LORD is your strength.

NEHEMIAH 8:10

As a widow, one of the greatest battles you may face is that of loneliness and grief. Whether the death of your mate is an expected loss or a sudden tragedy, the absence of his presence and familiar routine are continual reminders of your loss. This void can either swallow you up in its pain, or you can allow God's presence to fill this place with His healing.

As an insurance and financial investment consultant, I realized the difficulties many widows faced with the unexpected and often unprepared for death of their husbands. As if the emotional strain wasn't enough, many, I found, were not financially prepared for such a loss.

As a result of this, I purposed to reach out to this often overlooked segment of society and open my home to these women twice a year for a special time of ministry, fellowship, and support. One of these events is always on Valentine's Day—a day they would have typically shared with their mates—and I didn't want them to experience it alone.

I had enjoyed hosting these special luncheons for more than ten years. That is until February 7, 2001. On that day, my husband of thirty-one years was rushed to the hospital with what appeared to be a massive heart attack. He died a couple of days later, from what was discovered to be a defective gene. Now just one week before the annual widow's Valentine luncheon, ironically I found myself part of the same group of women I had determined to bless. I was a widow at age fifty-five.

To say the least, I was in shock. There was no time of preparation to adjust to his passing. One moment I was a happy wife with a loving husband, and the next I had joined the ranks of the very women I had been working to help.

With invitations already sent for the annual luncheon, I made the decision to continue as planned. I asked my assistant to call each of the women to let them know the event would proceed as usual. Just one week after the unexpected death of my husband, my home was filled with women in similar circumstances and I was ministering to their needs with a hug, fellowship, and comfort. I felt they needed me more than I needed not to do it.

The amazing thing was, I did not experience grief. I know that is hard to imagine, but it's true. Don't get me wrong, I loved my husband dearly. When he died I was in shock. But immediately I realized I had a choice. I thought, *Satan, you're not going to get my joy or get me down!* I knew from classes I had taken on assisting with hospice education that the bottom line in staying away from grief was to help others and get my mind off myself. So that is exactly what I began to do. I allowed myself to grieve for my husband, but I refused to allow myself to be *overcome* with grief. That's not to say there weren't opportunities, though.

One evening at the time when my husband and I would often sit and talk over our day, the depth of my loss came crashing in around me. I just wanted to sit and cry. But God spoke to my heart, *Don't go there, Earline. That will only produce depression.* When I made the decision not to give in to the emotion of grief, but instead began to sing and worship the Lord, that feeling immediately left me and has never returned.

You will have tears, but you don't have to have a heavy heart with the tears. Tears are for a season, but He wants to replace those tears with His joy.

Dear God, heal my broken heart and fill it with Your peace. Help me let go of my grief and exchange it for Your joy. Enable me to remember my mate with fondness, and dry all of my tears. You are my strength, oh Lord, and I put my trust in You. Amen.

FILLING THE DUAL ROLE OF MOTHER AND FATHER

Mary

I had fainted, unless I had believed to see the goodness of the LORD in the land of the living. Wait on the LORD: be of good courage, and he shall strengthen thine heart.

PSALM 27:13–14 KJV

The transition from marriage to widowhood can be even more difficult for those with young children. I know, because at age fifty I was left with a ten-year-old son and a twelve-year-old daughter to raise by myself after my husband died of colon cancer.

Overnight my world changed. Not only was I now the sole provider for our household, but I was also responsible for taking care of my mother who had just moved in with us after being diagnosed in the early stages of mental dementia.

But that was only the beginning of many challenges I would face in the coming days. With the loss of my husband, I was forced to return to full-time employment, which had a domino effect on other areas of our lives.

Once I returned to work, my daughter could no longer take dance classes. My son, who had previously been active in soccer, was forced to quit when I was no longer able to provide transportation to and from these activities due to my work schedule. Just getting them to school became an almost over-whelming task. When I worked the 7:00–3:00 P.M. shift at the local hospital where I was a pharmacist, I couldn't get them to school. When I worked the 3:00–11:00 P.M. shift, there was no one to pick them up. For a short time I was able to join a carpool, but eventually the other participants felt I wasn't con-tributing enough, and I was asked to drop out. It was a very difficult time of adjustment for all of us.

To complicate matters further, the economic situation in our community took a downward turn. Unable to make ends meet, I was forced to relocate to a new position in another city, taking a huge loss on the sale of our home due to the depressed economy. The pressures were incredible, but finally things began to change.

The relocation and new job brought a much-needed increase in pay, but the greatest blessing was that of our new church family. We began attending a church that was unlike any other I had ever attended. When the pastor preached, the glory of God filled the room. I had never been in meetings like that. I began to know God in a way I had never known Him before. Slowly He began to heal my heart through His power and glory that were in that little church. During this time when I had no husband, God became my husband and taught me to trust Him as never before.

Twenty years ago, I had no support group to help me through that difficult stage. I soon found that married friends didn't understand what I was going through; and although they meant well, they soon disappeared from my life, leaving me alone with the pain, grief, and challenges of a single parent. But when friends failed me, God did not, and He brought me to a small church family in Texas who knew the power of God.

If you are in the season of widowhood, God's Word promises that He will protect and provide for you. He is Jehovah Jireh, the God who sees ahead and makes provision for you as in the story of Abraham and Isaac.[16] God instructed Abraham to offer his son Isaac as a sacrifice, and Abraham promptly set out to obey. But God saw ahead, and at the very moment that Abraham was following through on God's directive, God provided a ram in the thicket to be sacrificed instead. Abraham was prepared to obey, but God saw ahead and provided the ram. Likewise, He sees your need even before You do, and He will provide what you need at just the right time.

As a body of believers, we are to assist the widows and the orphans. Look around you in your neighborhood, at church, in your family. There are those who need your assistance, whether it's a kind word, picking up a prescription for a widow who is sick, or baby-sitting so she can get her hair done. Your small sacrifice could help make someone's day.

Dear God, thank You for Your promise never to leave us nor forsake us. Even well-meaning people can let us down, but You never will. Heal our broken hearts, and give us grace to walk through this difficult time. Amen.

---

[16] See Genesis 22:1–14.

WOMEN OF THE BIBLE

Ruth[17]

*Boaz replied, "I've been told all about what you have done
for your mother-in-law since the death of your husband—
how you left your father and mother and your homeland
and came to live with a people you did not know before....
May you be richly rewarded by the LORD, the God of
Israel, under whose wings you have come to take refuge."*

RUTH 2:11–12

The book of Ruth provides a striking contrast as to the effects
loss and grief can play in our lives. The responses of Naomi and
Ruth to the tragedy of losing their husbands were completely
opposite in terms of their attitudes, outlook, and actions.

Naomi lost her husband followed soon after by the death of
both of her sons—devastating losses to be sure. In dealing with
them, Naomi embraced her grief stating, "Don't call me Naomi
... call me Mara ('Bitter'), because the Almighty has made my
life very bitter" (Ruth 1:20). True to the name she gave herself,
she became a bitter woman.

Ruth, on the other hand, also experienced a painful loss, that
of her husband—who happened to be one of Naomi's sons. With
her husband and provider dead, Ruth faced not only the loss of

---

[17] See the book of Ruth.

her mate, but fear regarding provision for her future. This is where Ruth's true character emerged. She could have returned to her own family who would have more than likely provided her with shelter and food—a safe and acceptable choice. Instead, however, she insisted on remaining with Naomi—a God choice. Her faithfulness, compassion, and loyalty to her mother-in-law soon gained the recognition of those around her.

Instead of allowing bitterness and sorrow to engulf her, Ruth immediately stretched out her hand to help someone else in need. In Ruth 2:7–12 we read that she was a hard worker who quickly gained the respect and favor of the other workers and ultimately the estate owner, Boaz. Her hard work, humble heart, and care for others above her own needs resulted in provision for both her and Naomi. Ultimately, she was rewarded with a new husband and family, establishing her in the lineage of Christ.

Dear God, help me to look past my own loss and needs to recognize others who are in pain around me, many of whom are hurting more than I am. Use me to minister to them, for I know that as I give out of my own need, You will abundantly provide for me. Amen.

LIFE LESSONS

1. It is possible to grieve without being overcome by grief.
2. Reaching out to someone else in need, rather than being consumed by your own pain, will result in healing.

3. If bitterness has made its way into your heart, ask God to remove it and heal you, so He can flood your heart with His joy.

4. Better days are ahead.

THE SUNSET YEARS

Evelyn Roberts

(AS TOLD TO KAREN HARDIN)

Moses was a hundred and twenty years old when he died,
yet his eyes were not weak nor his strength gone.

DEUTERONOMY 34:7

I've always said, it will be time to retire when the people
stop calling—and they haven't stopped yet. Today at the age of
eighty-five, I am still active in the ministry with my husband,
Oral. Twice a month we go to minister in various churches and
seminars, but one of the primary areas where I reach people
now is in my own community.

When I am out in my neighborhood taking a walk, my
neighbors often come up and tell me things like, "Evelyn, I don't
know if you have heard, but my daughter has cancer." They
don't necessarily ask me to pray, but I always do right then. I
don't ask; I just lay my hands on their shoulders, and we pray

for that situation, whatever it is. When I'm finished, they are always so appreciative.

There are also many who call on the phone requesting prayer. One dear lady has been a friend of ours for years. Whenever she gets down mentally, physically, or spiritually, she calls, and we pray with her. Not long ago she called me and said she was lying in bed, unable to move one of her legs. A visit to the doctor had garnered no specific reason as to the lame leg. His advice was simply, "Stay in bed." With her being ninety years of age, I knew she needed more medical advice than she had received, so I told her, "I am going to pray for you, and I want you to find another doctor who will tell you more about this situation."

The next morning I received another phone call, this time from the security guard at her apartment complex. He informed me that she had been hospitalized. The new doctor had discovered a blood clot and had immediately scheduled her for surgery. She came home two or three days later and called again. Although so weak she could barely speak, she wanted to express her appreciation for our prayers and said, "I know it is because of your prayers that I have made it."

"We are going to keep praying for you," I told her. "And you are going to come out of that bed." Every two or three days I continued to call to check on her progress, pray with her, and encourage her. She did recover completely and today is doing just fine.

I refer to these years as my harvest years after so many years of traveling in ministry and pouring our lives into the students at Oral Roberts University. God has blessed us, and we are seeing that blessing even now. My ministry personally has shifted mostly to prayer and encouragement and often a small joke to help bring joy such as the one I shared with our dear friend who had the blood clot. It goes something like this:

The Lord was talking with a man one day and said to him, "You know, you have been a good Christian all your life. You have obeyed Me in every area. I want to do something very special for you. What would you like?"

After some consideration, the man replied, "Lord, I have always wanted to go to Hawaii. But I don't like to fly, and I can't swim. Could you create a long bridge, so I can drive over?"

The Lord replied, "Son, this is a big request. Do you realize the length of the bridge and the depth of the piers that would be needed to complete this project? Isn't there something else you would like?"

"Well," said the man, "I've had four wives, and I have never understood any of them. Can you make me understand women?"

Without hesitation the Lord replied, "Now, how many lanes did you want on that bridge?"

A merry heart does good like a medicine, just like the Bible says. That is what we try to bring to others. There are always people around you who need help, and we are obligated and responsible to help those people whom the Lord sends our way.

People don't always make it easy for you, but He has given me such boldness that I am never embarrassed to pray, no matter where we are. Jesus said, "Whoever is ashamed of Me and My words, of him the Son of Man will be ashamed when He comes in His own glory, and in His Father's" (Luke 9:26 NKJV).

Not everyone is called to a pulpit ministry, but you can always help those you meet at the grocery store or who live next door. That's what Jesus would do.

Dear God, regardless of my age, I invite You to minister to others through me. Give me eyes to see the needs of those around me and boldness to reach out with an encouraging word and prayer. Amen.

EVELYN ROBERTS, wife of evangelist Oral Roberts, has been by his side in ministry for more than fifty years. She is the author of several books including, *His Darling Wife, Evelyn;* a children's book, *Heaven Has a Floor;* and *Evelyn Roberts' Miracle Life Stories.* The Roberts make their home in Newport Beach, California.

You're Never Too Old to Touch a Life in Need

Lois

*The LORD blessed the latter part of
Job's life more than the first.*

JOB 42:12

Widowed at only forty-nine years old, I knew there was
still much I could accomplish. At fifty-seven I enrolled in Bible
school, and later at sixty-seven, I enrolled in a missions training
program. For almost twenty-five years now, I have been
actively ministering in other countries, teaching in Bible schools,
preaching in local churches, praying for the sick, and distributing
Bibles. My life has been filled with incredible instances of God
touching others through me, just because I've been available.
Here is one such story:

Shortly after graduating from Bible school, I heard of a
ministry that went to university campuses to share the love of

Jesus with the students. I thought to myself, *I would love to do that, if only I were younger.* After receiving a letter from a friend regarding that ministry, I suddenly knew that this was God's next step for me. I applied shortly thereafter and was accepted.

I have often told people that my ministry at that time was what I called a "washroom ministry." Whenever I arrived on a campus, I would enter the bathroom and stand at the mirror combing my hair, waiting. As the female students would enter, I would ask each of them, "Have you ever asked Jesus into your heart?"

On one such occasion, a young lady entered, but I soon realized she couldn't speak English. Undeterred, I immediately repeated the question in French, at which point her eyes widened in surprise to hear her own language. I had discovered her language, but felt my own linguistic ability in French was too limited to carry on a complete conversation. Once again I asked the question, but this time in Spanish, my second language. "Have you ever asked Jesus into your heart?" Amazingly, the young woman could also speak Spanish, and I was able to share with her and lead her to the Lord—standing right there in the ladies' bathroom!

I have story after story of how God has graciously used me during these later years of my life. Since graduating from the missions school, I have traveled and ministered in the Philippines, Hong Kong, China, Costa Rica, Canada, England, Iceland, Scotland,

Mexico, Bolivia, Amsterdam, Russia, Israel, and Peru; and now at eighty-five, I am leaving for Jamaica in a few weeks. After that I am planning to return to Mexico and renew my Spanish, so that I can continue telling others of Christ's love there.

This is so much fun; people don't know what they're missing. It's so much easier to tell others about the Lord than you think it is. For all of this, God gets the glory. I could not have done any of it without Him.

Dear God, help me remember that Your plan for me is not dependent on my age and is not finished until You call me home. Forgive me for the times I have felt I was past the age of usefulness. Open my eyes to see opportunities to grow in You and be used by You. Strengthen me each day for Your service. Amen.

DIFFICULT
DECISIONS

Lenis

*I have fought the good fight, I have finished the race, I
have kept the faith. Now there is in store for me the crown
of righteousness, which the Lord, the righteous Judge,
will award to me on that day—and not only to me,
but also to all who have longed for his appearing.*

2 TIMOTHY 4:7–8

I don't think I made the decision to finally admit my
husband, Bill, into the nursing home. I listened to the voices of
my four children and their spouses who were repeatedly telling
me, "This is what you have to do, Mother. Your health is
beginning to deteriorate. You can't take care of him by yourself
any longer." It was heartbreaking, and it wasn't what I wanted
to do; but I knew the children were right.

After forty–three years of marriage, Bill and I had been
looking forward to the upcoming years as his retirement drew
near. Prior to retirement, Bill began to put his dreams into
motion and purchased a camping trailer, excited at the prospect

that we would finally have the time to travel. We had both enjoyed good health throughout our marriage and had no reason to believe that things would change.

But they did and very quickly.

The day after he retired, Bill was involved in an automobile accident. Although he was only dazed from the crash, it signaled a change. While there were no major injuries from the collision, the trauma acted as a catalyst, ending his previously good health. From that time on, he began to experience continual health challenges including dementia. Over the next six years as his health declined and difficulties surfaced, numerous tests were run. The doctors finally diagnosed a brain tumor about the size of a quarter behind his left ear. They recommended its removal, advising us that the tumor would continue to grow if left on its own. It was a difficult decision because it involved the brain, but the doctors seemed confident that they could easily remove the tumor with no side effects. After much consideration and prayer, we finally decided to have the tumor removed.

But the surgery didn't go well. Once the doctors were inside, they discovered that the tumor was between the brain stem and the facial nerve. The surgery became complicated. In the end, they were able to extricate the tumor, but only after damaging the facial nerve.

It was devastating. Bill was in severe pain for the first five to six days after the surgery. When he had finally recovered enough to come home, he was severely

limited in what he could do and remained in bed most of the time. It was difficult for us both. He struggled with his inability to do things, and I struggled with the enormous task of his constant care.

Bill slowly began to recover, but there were more obstacles ahead—bladder surgery, treatments for prostate cancer, and a series of small strokes. We were now in our seventies, and it was becoming more and more difficult for me to perform the constant and heavy task of his care.

When it finally became clear that a change had to be made, our next challenge was to find the right facility. A brief stay at two recommended homes was unsatisfactory, the second ending abruptly after he fell out of bed and was injured.

It was past midnight when we got him into the emergency room after the fall. His arm had been injured, and doctors were pessimistic about his chances of recovery, not only regarding the injured arm, but about his overall health.

"He won't get any better. It will be downhill from here on," they told us that night. But I knew God had a better plan.

"I don't think so," I boldly told the doctor. "I'm a Christian, and I'm going to trust the Lord."

After Bill was released from the hospital, he returned to the nursing home, but it was quickly evident that another solution had to be found. That is when we saw God work a miracle.

Bill wanted to get into the Veteran's Center, but after calling we learned that there was a long waiting list. They were uncertain how long it would be before a room might open, estimating anywhere from six months to a year! Undaunted, however, I called the next week to inquire again, only to hear once more that Bill's name was "way down on the waiting list." Then to my surprise, I got a call the very next day informing me of an open room. It was a miracle, which we accepted immediately.

The last five years have been such an improvement over our initial struggle to find a good nursing home. Bill is receiving such wonderful care and is doing so much better. I am able to rest because I know he is being well taken care of, and he is happily content and settled into a comfortable routine. In our time together now, we just enjoy being together and looking back over the years.

Through it all I have remained involved with a women's Bible study group, assisted with the landscaping needs of my daughter and son-in-law's business, and developed a relationship with my young grandchildren. These are things I do because I enjoy them, even though my kids gets concerned that I am overdoing things.

"Do you want your mother to just sit down and die? That is what will happen if she doesn't stay busy," the doctor informed them.

And so I have stayed busy and plan to do so as long as I am able, because I know that God will see me through.

Dear God, sometimes difficult seasons are thrust upon us, but even then You show Yourself strong on our behalf. Help me to always recognize You in the midst of my trials, and give me the wisdom I need to navigate through these troubled times safely and with Your blessing. Make a way where there seems to be no way. Amen.

WOMEN OF THE BIBLE

Anna[18]

*There was also a prophetess, Anna, the daughter of
Phanuel, of the tribe of Asher. She was very old;
she had lived with her husband seven years after
her marriage, and then was a widow until she
was eighty-four. She never left the temple but
worshiped night and day, fasting and praying.*

LUKE 2:36–37

Although Anna is mentioned in the Bible only once, and briefly
at that, we learn volumes regarding her faithfulness and dedication to
the Lord. Anna was a prophetess. Married only seven years when
she became a widow, she then dedicated herself completely to
worship, fasting, and prayer in the temple. She so completely gave
herself to this ministry that the Bible says she remained in the temple
day and night. But it was not until she was eighty-four years old that
her most notable act occurred—that of prophetically acknowledging
the deity of Jesus when His parents brought Him to the temple.

Anna was a woman of character. Although in her sunset
years, she chose to make a difference. Because of her years of dedication, she had developed a deep sensitivity to the things of God
so that when she met Mary, Joseph, and the baby Jesus in the

---

[18] See Luke 2:36–38.

162

temple, she immediately began to prophesy over Jesus, pointing the way to His work as the Messiah. Anna's years of quiet, unnoticed service to the Lord prepared her for this most outstanding moment of her life, a moment recorded for all time. All because she stayed dedicated to God, throughout the remainder of her life.

Dear God, during my sunset years, the main thing I want to do is to know You more by spending time with You. I make myself available to be used by You in any way You see fit. Whether my remaining years are spent in the public eye or in my prayer closet, may my life serve to point others to You. Amen.

LIFE LESSONS

1. Let Jesus be Lord over your autumn years, seeking His will for this season of your life.

2. You can impact those around you by simply offering an encouraging word, a hug, or a prayer.

3. Continued service to God is not based on age but availability.

The Grace of

Winter

A
MOTHER'S LOSS

Cheryl Prewitt-Salem[19]

My soul finds rest in God alone; my salvation comes
from him. He alone is my rock and my salvation;
he is my fortress, I will never be shaken.

PSALM 62:1–2

The death of a child, no matter at what age, has to be one of the deepest pains anyone experiences. No one can possibly comprehend it until he or she has walked through it, and not one experience is exactly the same as another. There is an old saying that goes something like this: "Never judge a man until you have walked a mile in his shoes." My husband, Harry, and I appreciate this saying so much more since we walked through the most painful time of our lives. We now have compassion for those who are caretakers and/or have experienced the death of someone they love. We also have a deeper appreciation for what our heavenly Father did when He sent His own Son to be sacrificed for our sins.

---

[19] Excerpt reprinted with permission. Cheryl Prewitt–Salem, *From Mourning to Morning* (Tulsa, OK: Harrison House Publishers) copyright © 2001, pp. 65, 137, 139, 263.

When we were told that our daughter, Gabrielle Christian Salem, had an inoperable brain tumor, our world turned upside down. The doctors gave us two months, but Gabrielle fought the fight and ran the race for eleven months and twelve days. She made a choice on November 23, 1999, to leave the shell she was in, to leave the stretch marks, the stripes on her body, behind. At 7:05 A.M. her little paralyzed face relaxed, her breathing changed from short quick breaths to normal breathing. She began blowing through sweet, puckered lips like she was kissing the angels around her as she left with her heavenly escort.

It is unnatural for a parent to have to bury a child. It doesn't line up with the scheme of life. It begets grief beyond comprehension, but it is not without hope for those who are in Christ Jesus. The Word is very specific about this, as it says in this Scripture:

"Now also we would not have you ignorant, brethren, about those who fall asleep [in death], that you may not grieve [for them] as the rest do who have no hope [beyond the grave]" (1 Thess. 4:13 AMP). People come up to us all the time and ask how we have been able to bear the pain. Our only answer is that our hope is in the Lord. We know where Gabrielle is, and we know she is fully restored.

The Lord showed us that grief and death are twin-rooted spirits. Death comes and goes quickly, but grief stays if we let it. The spirit of grief does not come from God. That means it comes from Satan, and it can be deadly because it attacks your emotions and sucks the very Word—life and breath—of God out of you.

When you live in "tornado alley," as we do in Oklahoma, you learn a lot about tornadoes. The worst kind of tornado is one that goes along a path and spins off a twin. The twin is more violent, unpredictable, and destructive than the original storm. Grief is like a tornado that sweeps down sucking every-thing in its path up into the funnel cloud spinning off a twin, that is death. That is why grief is such a dangerous place.

Gabrielle's graduation was earlier than we expected or wanted it to be. At six years old, she had accomplished more for God's kingdom than most do in a lifetime. Maybe that is why she went so soon. We are comforted in knowing where she is and that she is completely restored, and when our work on this earth is over we will be with her again.

Dear God, there are days I wake up and simply want to close my eyes again to shut out the constant reminder of our loss. In these times, wrap the arms of Your presence around me and comfort me. I don't know how You will do it, but somehow, God, let me use what I learn in this season to minister to others. Amen.

CHERYL SALEM grew up in Choctaw County, Mississippi, and overcame many challenges to become Miss America 1980. She, along with husband, Harry, and two sons, Harry III and Roman, make up Salem Family Ministries as they travel extensively throughout the United States ministering God's love and healing for the hurting. Cheryl is an accomplished speaker, musician, recording artist, teacher, and author and has written such books as *A Bright Shining Place* and *The Mommy Book*.

JESUS IS
MAKING
MY BED

Charlotte

When the perishable has been clothed with the
imperishable, and the mortal with immortality, then the
saying that is written will come true: "Death has been
swallowed up in victory." "Where, O death, is your
victory? Where, O death, is your sting?"

1 CORINTHIANS 15:54–55

When I reflect on the past twenty-nine years, I don't know
that it ever really hit me that my child wasn't going to be an
adult. You just try to live your life as normally as possible and
make the most of every moment.

My husband, Ed, and I never really knew normal. Our first
child, Jeffrey, was born, followed two and a half years later by
his twin sisters, Jennifer and Karin. That's when the word
"normal" could no longer define our family. Fraternal twins,

Karin was a typical healthy baby, but something was very different about her sister, Jennifer.

Jennifer was sick from day one. There were always colds, coughing, and various ailments. Although she was sick a lot, she wasn't sick enough to really merit the doctor's full concern. After running a few tests, most doctors felt that her symptoms were allergy induced. Their recommendation was to wait until she was a little older to conduct more extensive testing to pinpoint trigger elements. But I knew it was something more. Jenn wasn't flourishing as my other children. She was malnourished and coughed all the time. Finally out of total frustration, I called the doctor and said, "Do something with me or her; I can't take it anymore."

When Jennifer was nearly three, the doctor finally agreed to begin allergen testing. What was supposed to be one full day in the local hospital turned into a thirty-six-day nightmare as doctors continued to search for the root cause of Jenn's physical condition. We were not prepared for what the doctor would tell us.

I remember clearly the day of the diagnosis as we sat in the noisy medical clinic, almost twenty-eight years ago. My husband held Jenn on his lap next to me with the doctor on my other side. Even at such close proximity, I had to strain to hear the doctor's quiet words, which would forever echo in my ears, "Your daughter has cystic fibrosis and will probably only live to her twenty-first birthday."

Cystic fibrosis is an inherited condition that produces thick mucus particularly in the lungs of its victims, preventing normal breathing. Most CF patients are malnourished because the effort to breath—a function that the average person takes for granted—requires such enormous energy that it consumes a large number of calories. Breathing treatments, bronchial drainage, chest physical therapy, up to twenty different medications all became a normal part of our daily routine. There was little time to ponder the magnitude of the diagnosis in the midst of this new activity. Our entire family now revolved around the needs and treatments necessary to keep Jenn breathing.

In retrospect, there were positive steps we took because of the diagnosis. We chose to make a lot of memories, taking regular family vacations and going on outings that more than likely would have been postponed had the clock not been ticking against us. These were special times that can never be replaced. I wonder how often many families with healthy children miss such opportunities because of the busyness of daily life.

Jenn never let her illness hold her back from living as normal a life as possible. She was active in school and had lots of friends. After graduating from high school, she enrolled in the University of South Carolina to obtain her degree in insurance management. It was around this time that her dad was transferred to another city. Discussing the impending move as a family, our children chose to remain in Columbia—the city where they had been raised—to complete their education and be with friends. It was difficult moving so far away, but I also knew that Jenn was old enough to make this decision. She was doing well in school and managing the disease. We were all hopeful.

Two years later, while out with her brother and a group of friends, Jenn began to feel very ill. Her brother immediately drove her to the hospital where they discovered she had a collapsed lung. It was a very painful and frightening experience. I found out later, it was also a turning point in our fight against the dreaded outcome.

"Mom, I have eighteen months left," Jenn stated pragmatically, shortly after her release from the hospital. Having done her own research of the disease over the years, she had read that a collapsed lung was a signal of final deterioration. Six weeks later at age twenty-three, she experienced her second collapsed lung. Again, she was able to rally from this painful period and resumed many of her normal activities, with only a few new restrictions.

Not long after, she decided to join her father and me in Tulsa. Each night before bed, we went through a lengthy process of hooking her up to an IV; a feeding tube, which had finally been inserted to combat her weakening condition and her usual dose of medications; breathing treatments; and oxygen. But even with these added inconveniences, Jenn never complained.

The last time Jenn went to the hospital was for a rather routine procedure to clear her lungs. The doctors expected her to be in and out within a couple of days, but once in the hospital her condition deteriorated and her breathing became even more labored than normal.

Alone with her in the hospital room that night, I must have dosed when all of a sudden she sat up in bed and said, "I'm going to see Grandma and Jesus." I went over to stand next to the bed, and she said to me very clearly, "You need to get a pencil and paper." I looked around and amazingly found a clipboard full of paper that had been left sitting on the windowsill. Grabbing it I began to take notes as Jenn shared with me specific requests for her funeral and who she wanted to receive some of her more prized possessions. It was such a surreal moment, hearing my daughter essentially share with me her last will and testament. What do you say in such a moment? After she completed her list, I asked her, "Do you want the funeral to be here or back in Columbia?" She looked at me with a sweet smile and said, "You know, Mom, it really doesn't matter."

I knew at that moment that for her, it really didn't matter. She had already left this world in her heart and was preparing for the next. It was 2:00 A.M. when we finished the list and I called my husband. "Jenn's ready to go see Jesus. You need to come now."

Karin was in town, and by the time she and my husband arrived, Jenn's labored breathing had relaxed and she was resting peacefully. It looked as if her hair and face were literally glowing. As Ed and Karin entered the room, she acknowledged their presence without even opening her eyes by saying, "I love you so much, but Jesus is making my bed." Those were her final words as she slipped into a coma, dying a few hours later.

Returning from the hospital, I entered Jenn's room still full of the medical paraphernalia, which had been the norm for practically her entire life. For the first time, I opened her prayer journal, which she had begun almost two years before when her lung collapsed the first time. It revealed the heart of a young woman not caught up in her own problems, but one more concerned with those of others. Entry after entry chronicled her joyful spirit, "Thank You, God, for helping me in rehab today." "Thank You for giving me strength." There was only one entry in the entire journal in which she requested relief from the constant pain in her lungs.

There were also entries in which she was praying for people we didn't know, and from what I gathered, she must have heard about their plight via the television or radio. Even though her physical activities had become more restricted toward the end, her prayers had reached beyond her own limitations as she became a prayer warrior championing the needs of others.

Jenn's twin, Karin, wrote a letter recently about her sister's life, which was used in an fund-raiser to find a cure for CF. Her letter began, "My sister had an awesome life." I thought about it a moment and had to agree. In her twenty-five brief years with us, Jennifer Ann Hartung had an awesome life. Her life touched many people, and we are all better for it.

Dear God, the loss of a child is almost unbearable. I need Your strength to get up each day and go on with life. Even though it doesn't feel like it now, I know my life will go on because You have a plan for me. Help me to recognize it, so I can move forward. Amen.

THE LOSS OF
A PARENT

Karen Hardin

*Even though I walk through the valley of the shadow
of death, I will fear no evil, for you are with me;
your rod and your staff, they comfort me.*

PSALM 23:4

The stories on loss have unquestionably been the most difficult of this book. Personal friends who have experienced the loss of children were the initial focus of this chapter until the reality of further loss touched my own world and opened a different season in my life—the loss of a parent.

My oldest brother didn't phone often. After exchanging greetings, he immediately cut to the purpose of his call. "Dad has cancer," he stated almost pragmatically, emotionless. The brief conversation ended with little further information, leaving me with a multitude of unanswered questions. I was shaken. It was the first time I had really had to consider my parent's mortality, and I didn't like it.

Just two years before, my husband and I had experienced the loss of four grandparents within a six-month period. All in their eighties, their passing was inevitable, but the sudden loss of all remaining grandparents within such a short time frame was extremely difficult. It also ushered us into a new position as our parents were now the oldest members still living in the family lineage. I quickly dismissed the uncomfortable thought from my mind, unwilling to travel that road of thought to its inevitable conclusion. If our grandparents had lived into their eighties, then it was highly probable that there were still lots of fruitful years left with our parents who were all in good health, I rationalized.

I was wrong.

I called my father to see how he was doing. "So what did the doctor say?" I asked, hoping for some sort of assurance from the ugly threat that had invaded our lives.

"Oh, Nadine (my stepmom) says I can't die now or she'll kill me," he quipped, trying to keep the tone light. "They don't know for sure how widespread the cancer is, so they have ordered more tests."

After disconnecting, I spent another hour on the Internet researching the disease, medical and nutritional treatments, effects, and life expectancy. While our family believed in the power of prayer and healing, I also wanted to be as educated as possible about what lay before us. The information I found was both helpful and hopeful. His form of cancer was one that when diagnosed early was often treatable.

When I visited Dad a few weeks later, I was unprepared for the change that had already taken place. Arriving at the insurance agency my father owned, I was directed by the receptionist to the back part of the building, which was actually my dad and Nadine's home. The receptionist said he was resting. I was surprised. It was the middle of the day and completely uncharacteristic of my workaholic father to be resting. As I walked into the living room, I found him lying on the sofa, covered with a blanket. He looked tired, frail, and very still.

"Hi, Dad. It's me," I said as I knelt beside him, trying to disguise the shock I felt from his changed appearance. He kept his eyes closed for most of my short visit, the effort to open them obviously requiring more strength than he possessed. I prayed with him and got up to leave when he finally spoke.

"I'm not ready to go yet. Not this soon," he said softly in a voice that trembled. The calm composure I had struggled to maintain through the visit crumbled instantly as we both faced the harsh reality of his quickly deteriorating condition. Without a miracle he would soon be gone.

Over the next few months, my dad endured hormone treatments, radiation treatments, and together we explored the untypical and sometimes less than appealing nutritional avenues for help. As I continued searching the Scriptures regarding God's Word on healing, I would fax Dad page after page of verses for his own spiritual growth and prayer. He began to regain his strength and appetite, and after a few weeks returned to a too full schedule at the office. We were all encouraged by this tremendous turnaround. But it didn't last for long.

"Hi, Dad. It's Karen," I said as our previously infrequent contact increased to a weekly regularity. Neither one of us enjoyed phone conversations as our primary form of communication, choosing notes and letters as our preferred medium of correspondence. Although we lived just over ten miles apart, our relationship up until a few years before had been distant. My parents' divorce twenty-five years earlier had greatly affected the depth of our relationship, particularly in the realm of communication. However, when my husband and I had relocated to China, Dad's and my distant relationship began to grow as he faithfully jotted down his thoughts and ideas, sending letters every couple of days.

It was odd, but halfway around the world, I was finally getting to know my dad. Although we had since returned to the States, our letter writing continued. Even during the sickness, we continued with short notes and E-mails, which allowed us frequent contact until his condition deteriorated further and his fingers would no longer cooperate to hold a pen or type a note. At that time, we resorted to the more typical phone calls to stay in contact, but even these were no longer possible as his speech began to slur due to the effects of the increased pain medication.

Father's Day was approaching as the doctors predicted his remaining life to be only a matter of days. *How ironic,* I thought, as the family gathered around the hospital bed, now erected in what had been his living room, to wish him for the last time a happy Father's Day. As the rest of the family filed out, my husband and I were the last ones to bend down and kiss his cheek. As we did, he tried to say something, but his words were too difficult to understand. Obviously frustrated, he pointed to the faithful pen and paper, which had served us so well over the years to communicate his message. Tears blurred my vision as he struggled, unable to control the instrument that had bridged the gap in our relationship, providing a means of communication and a deeper relationship.

We received the call at the end of the week. Dad was finally out of pain. Although he had not been healed in the way I had hoped, over the years our relationship had. Even now on my desk are reminders as small yellow Post-It notes with Dad's familiar scribble are scattered in various areas of my workplace: "Good job," "I love you," "Thought you might be interested."

I smile at the notes and am reminded of the verse, "Precious in the sight of the LORD is the death of his saints" (Ps. 116:15). Dad has simply transitioned into his final, but glorious season with the Lord, and I draw comfort knowing that I will one day see him again.

Dear God, guide me beside still waters and restore my soul. Heal my pain and dry my tears. Let me feel Your embrace and peace during the days ahead. Amen.

WOMEN OF THE BIBLE

Rizpah[20]

Cast your burden on the LORD, and He shall sustain you;
He shall never permit the righteous to be moved.

PSALM 55:22 NKJV

Two of Rizpah's sons had been taken from her and put to death. Because they were of the lineage of Saul, their blood and that of their half brothers had been required to break the famine in the land spawned from God's judgment against Saul's actions. With no warning, her sons were handed over to the Gibeonites who "killed and exposed them on a hill before the LORD" (2 Sam. 21:9). While this act was necessary to reverse the curse over the land spiritually, it did nothing to assuage the heartache and loss of a mother for her sons.

Whether due to accident, sickness, or violence, the death of a child prior to the parents' passing can wreak devastation upon those left behind if they remain in the "land of the dead," so to speak.

Rizpah was so overcome with grief that she remained beside the bodies of her sons to prevent their inevitable destruction from the birds and wild animals. She chose to remain with the dead.

Compare her actions with those of King David.[21] His response to the loss of his illegitimate son with Bathsheba is

---

[20] See 2 Samuel 21:7–14.

[21] See 2 Samuel 12:11–24.

contrary to human nature, but comes from a heart that in grief could trust in the God of all comfort.

Second Samuel 12:19–21 says, "David noticed that his servants were whispering among themselves and he realized the child was dead.... Then David got up from the ground. After he had washed, put on lotions and changed his clothes, he went into the house of the LORD and worshiped. Then he went to his own house, and at his request they served him food, and he ate. His amazed servants asked him, 'Why are you acting this way? While the child was alive, you fasted and wept, but now that the child is dead, you get up and eat!'"

Immediately after the child's death David took four steps.

1. He got up and washed himself.

2. He worshiped the Lord.

3. He ate, resuming typical daily activities.

4. He comforted Bathsheba, the child's mother.

David recognized the important truth that to remain in the land of the dead could achieve no purpose other than further destruction. Did he grieve? Absolutely. But he understood that healing comes in the presence of the Lord.

He also understood that at the loss of their child, Bathsheba was grieving as well. Instead of isolation, David chose consolation, that as parents they could join together in the difficult healing process ahead.

Dear God, I don't see how I can return from the land of the dead and join the land of the living again, but I know with You, all things are possible. Give me the grace to be able to follow David's example and move on from this place. Amen.

LIFE LESSONS

1. Do not run from God in isolation, but to God for consolation; only He can bring true comfort for an aching heart.

2. To remain with the dead produces no lasting results. It only delays the inevitable—at some point you must move on.

3. Worship in such moments is a true sacrifice, but by it, supernatural healing for the soul can begin.

THE PAIN OF INFERTILITY

Twila Paris[22]

*Do not be anxious about anything, but in everything,
by prayer and petition, with thanksgiving, present
your requests to God. And the peace of God,
which transcends all understanding, will guard
your hearts and your minds in Christ Jesus.*

PHILIPPIANS 4:6–7

We didn't struggle with infertility in the classic sense; we struggled over other health concerns.

My husband, Jack, started to show symptoms right after we got engaged. He'd always been really healthy. We just thought he was having one of those years in which you get a bug and then you keep having setbacks and never quite get over it. So we didn't think much about it. But then the year after our

---

[22] Reprinted with permission. Ginger Kolbaba, *Today's Christian Woman* magazine (Carol Stream, IL: Christianity Today) May/June 2002.

wedding, he was still getting sick ... a lot. Finally, he went for some tests. The only thing the physicians could call it was chronic fatigue syndrome. He wasn't diagnosed with hepatitis C until almost a decade after his symptoms first appeared.

As a result of Jack's chronic illness, our physicians advised us not to try to get pregnant. So we didn't really have the option to try to get pregnant for a long time. Then a few years ago, after we met with a Christian nutritionist who helped us with diet, exercise, and supplements, Jack's health improved dramatically. At the same time, research data came in on the risk potential, and our physicians said it was okay if we wanted to try to have a baby.

That was a step of faith for us. Of course, I'd been praying about having a baby for years. But by the time we were actually able to try, I was 41 and at the point of praying, "God, at this stage in our lives, I'm not going to assume this is the best thing. You know our hearts. Please do what You know is best. We trust You with this."

Years earlier I'd had to commit my childlessness to God. I was about 35 when it hit me that having a baby may never happen. Most of the time I was okay with that thought. I was busy. God had given me wonderful things to do, and I loved my husband. But then sadness would hit me out of the blue. I'd see a baby, or a TV commercial, or a sweet outfit in the girls' department in a store, and then I'd feel depressed. I'd watched friends in difficult situations react with humility, and I'd watched others react with bitterness. So I stepped back and thought, *Which of those people do I want to become if this is my life?* I knew I didn't want to end up bitter.

I wasn't able to surrender my desires for a child overnight. God continually had to pour His grace into my life. But I knew I was finally okay when my sister Starla announced she was pregnant, and I was able to rejoice with her. That, to me, was clear evidence God had helped me resolve the issue.

A few months after my sister made her announcement, I decided to do the Lullaby project. About four weeks after I finished writing those lullabies, I found out I was pregnant! I'm not saying God said, "Do this project and then I'll give you a baby." But I don't know how to explain its timing. On some level it seems so like God, so gracious of Him to give us a baby when we'd been waiting all these years, and for that baby to be healthy when there were added risks. As if that's not enough, God first gave me the opportunity to write lullabies, which as far as I knew were for other people's children. To find out I was expecting a child almost literally to the moment I finished writing those lullabies shows God's attention to detail, His extra touch. I'm amazed God would take the time to work that way in our lives.

I didn't plan for my life to turn out this way—and neither did Jack. But I've discovered everybody has some area in her life in which she's saying, "Wait. This wasn't the dream."

When I was grappling with having children, I prayed, "Lord, look how old I am, and I don't have children yet. My children should have been in second grade by now. Look how old all my friends' children are. I'm a planner. I want to know what's going to happen and when." I think a lot of women are that way. But several months before J. P. was born, I felt God say, "I have a timetable, too, and Mine's more accurate."

I'm learning God's ultimately more interested in developing eternal character. He's willing to sacrifice our temporary happiness in order to bring us eternal joy. Remember, God sees the big picture. When I think about who He is and how He takes care of us, I realize God really is in control.

Dear God, I commit the whole area of infertility to You. You are the One who made us, and when there's something wrong, You're the One who can make things right. You know our desire for a little one, to pour our love into, to teach Your ways. I entrust this situation to Your care and ask You to grant our hearts' desire. Amen.

TWILA PARIS, her husband Jack, and J. P. make their home in Arkansas. Her children's album, *Bedtime Prayers: Lullabies and Peaceful Worship,* is currently available in Christian bookstores.

YOU'RE WASTING YOUR TIME

Sherry

*He settles the barren woman in her home
as a happy mother of children.*

PSALM 113:9

"We got the test results back. I want to tell you to stop
wasting your time and money and go on with your life without
children and be happy." These were the words the fertility spe‑
cialist spoke to us two years ago after the failure of our first in
vitro attempt. How many other couples have heard these same
words, or something similar?

If this sounds like you, take heart. We can tell you from
experience, *don't give up on your heart's desire.* We could have
given up in discouragement and failure. Instead, though, we turned
our efforts completely toward adoption, which we had already
begun to pursue. But things didn't go exactly as we expected.

Steve and I married later in life, consequently we didn't
want to wait too long before starting our family. Since my

husband is a quadriplegic, from an automobile accident before his senior year in high school, we were concerned that there might be some difficulty in achieving pregnancy. These concerns were put to rest when we learned I was pregnant a year and a half later. We were ecstatic. It didn't seem like things could get any better. That's when it all took a nosedive. Just four weeks into the pregnancy, we lost the baby. It was heartbreaking. But to make matters worse, four years later, I still hadn't been able to conceive again.

Realizing we weren't getting any younger, we finally took the initial steps to determine the cause of the infertility. We learned I had not one, but three major fertility issues, any of which single-handedly could prevent pregnancy. After receiving the diagnosis, I just cried. Our thoughts of family had always included children, and it seemed our dream was slipping away before our eyes.

The specialist eventually started me on fertility drugs and an attempt at artificial insemination. However, after two attempts they discovered I had severe endometriosis, and so all efforts had to be put on hold while I began treatments to get that condition under control. Eventually we had five unsuccessful attempts at artificial insemination over the next two to three years. It was an emotional roller coaster as the fertility hormone drugs propelled my emotions sky high, only to bring them crashing down a few days later. It didn't help that at this same time, *thirteen* of my friends were all pregnant! It seemed everyone was pregnant but me.

After these initial attempts, we then proceeded to the more expensive and complicated procedure of in vitro. Steve and I determined prior to the attempt that no matter what the outcome, successful or not, we would only do the procedure once.

I had to endure another round of fertility drugs, procedures, and emotional ups and downs to prepare my body for the highest probability of success. The procedure itself was a three-day process where the doctor first harvested my eggs. This stage was successful with five healthy eggs ready for the next stage. We learned later that after the introduction of the sperm, three of the eggs died immediately, leaving only two remaining. However, the doctor encouraged us that these looked good, and we continued with hopeful optimism. The night before we were to return to the clinic for the eggs to be reinserted into my womb, we received a call from the doctor. The remaining two eggs had died. The procedure was over and with it our hopes for pregnancy.

It was then that I realized I had been putting my trust in the fertility procedures instead of God. I repented right then, giving Him my desire for children. It was now in His hands.

We put off a required consultation with our fertility specialist for about three months after the failure of the in vitro procedure, feeling it would be only a formality rather than informative since we had already determined that we would not continue to pursue additional fertility measures. In spite of this, we were not prepared for the harsh reality of the doctor's diagnosis.

Who is ever prepared to hear such finality regarding a dream? Thankfully, we had already begun the necessary paperwork to be considered as adoptive parents. Where the doctor's words could have been devastating, they only confirmed our previous decision to cease fertility treatments and move forward with adoption. Over the next three weeks, we completed our home study. The only step remaining was to complete the paperwork necessary for the adoption process. Once again our excitement began to build as we rested in the knowledge that our trust was planted firmly in the Lord for our children.

We did get our child, but much quicker than we ever thought possible when we learned a few weeks later from a home pregnancy test that I was pregnant! Even more remarkable was that although we didn't know it at the time, I was already pregnant the day the fertility specialist pronounced we had no hope of conception in our future. In spite of the doctor's diagnosis, we not only conceived and had a beautiful baby girl, but it was almost exactly nine months after that fateful doctor's visit when we were told such a conception was impossible. Not only was it possible with God, but our *second* child, Alexis Mae, was born in May 2003.

Dear God, I know that You are the God of the impossible. When I begin to stagger and my faith becomes weak, help me take hold of Your unfailing promises and faithfulness. Amen.

THE MIRACLE BOY

Linda

*My tears have been my food day and night, while
men say to me all day long, "Where is your God?"
These things I remember as I pour out my soul: how I
used to go with the multitude, leading the procession to the
house of God, with shouts of joy and thanksgiving among
the festive throng. Why are you downcast, O my soul?
Why so disturbed within me? Put your hope in God,
for I will yet praise him, my Savior and my God.*

PSALM 42:3–6

It's been over fifteen years now, and doctors have never
been able to pinpoint the reason for our inability to conceive.
"Unexplained infertility" is the only explanation we were ever
given after years of surgery, tests, and fertility treatments
ranging from artificial insemination to five in vitro cycles. All of
these resulted in early miscarriages or failed attempts, an emotionally and financially draining experience.

My husband, Keith, and I had been married almost five years before we were finally able to admit that something was wrong. We contacted a specialist and began the grueling process of testing, treatments, and fertility drugs, which left my physical body swollen as if pregnant and my emotions in constant turmoil.

I tried to keep a positive outlook on life, but it was difficult attending baby showers and baptisms for other couples who had achieved our dream. When my friends would become pregnant, our family shielded us from the news. Although they meant well, not including us in their joy brought a pain all its own. If I couldn't rejoice with others, I felt I might never have a chance to rejoice at all.

Finally, Keith and I began to discuss the possibility of adoption. While this posed no issue in my heart, Keith not only expressed his hesitancy about adopting, but questioned our families' ability to accept such a child. Since we weren't in agreement, we didn't pursue it any further, but returned again to the now familiar cycle of fertility drugs and treatments.

This cycle continued until we approached a major milestone. We had now been married fifteen years. While age had not been a factor at the start of this process, it was becoming a more major player with each passing year. Time was running out. It was about this same time that an individual we both knew and deeply respected shared with Keith, "It takes a bigger man to love another man's child than to love your own." With this word, Keith's concerns regarding adoption gradually began to change.

We were finally ready to take the next step with one requirement—the adoption had to be closed. Years of dashed hopes and miscarriages had created fragile emotions. We both knew we could not withstand the additional stress of an open adoption and possible change of heart. We had just begun our investigation into a couple of agencies when God coordinated a divine appointment.

An acquaintance who knew nothing about our personal struggle for children walked into my office one day with the most amazing announcement: "I know a couple in their midforties who have just discovered the wife is pregnant. Already with several grown and older children, they were shocked with this new development. After much prayer, they feel God has shown them that this child is a gift for someone else. They are putting the baby up for adoption. Are you interested?"

My heart was pounding as she completed her news. "The family has one primary condition. It must be a closed adoption."

The timing and specifics hardly seemed a coincidence. Cautiously optimistic, I gave her the name of our lawyer so that a dialogue could begin. Returning home that night, Keith and I prayed over this miraculous opportunity. But was it our opportunity? As I shared the news with a close friend for prayer, she spoke this word, "This will be such a simple process that its very simplicity will be a confirmation to you that the child is yours."

Later that evening, we learned the couple had talked with our attorney for more than three hours. He called us with the following report, "This will be the simplest adoption I have ever done."

I knew then that this was our child.

The adoption proceeded with incredible speed. Now all we had to do was wait for the baby to be born. Four months later, we received the long-awaited call from our attorney. "The baby has been born, but there are complications. I will call you back."

It was 3:00 P.M. We immediately began calling everyone we knew to pray for the child we had yet to meet. We anxiously waited by the phone the remainder of the day, praying and wondering what was happening. The hours ticked away slowly, but our lawyer never called back. Finally, at midnight we could wait no longer and made a phone call of our own, reaching the owner of the law firm where our attorney worked.

"Look, I have a baby that's been born, and we've been told there are complications. I just want to know, is the baby dead or alive?"

Because it was a closed adoption and we didn't know the case number, the man had difficulty locating contact information. However, within an hour, we received a return call, "The child is alive," he said. That was all we knew until the following morning when our attorney finally called us back.

"We need to meet this morning and discuss what has happened," was all our attorney would share until we arrived at his office. As we took our seats, he handed us pictures taken that morning. Horrible pictures of a nine-pound fourteen-ounce baby that was so swollen he hardly resembled a baby at all. The doctors had had to perform an emergency C-section. Unknown at the time, the mother's placenta had ruptured, causing a severe loss of blood. It was a miracle either one had survived.

At the time of birth, the baby's organs had already begun to shut down. His blood pressure was 40, his heart rate 190, and his lungs weren't producing the chemicals necessary to function, putting him in severe respiratory distress. At birth he was immediately attached to life support. As they worked to stabilize his heart rate and blood pressure, they discovered that in addition to all of the above complications, he also had several holes in his heart.

Bringing the conversation back to the present, the lawyer asked us the ultimate question, "Basically we need to know if you still want the baby." The pictures before us were overwhelming. Had we come this far to lose yet another child?

Our "simple" adoption had turned into a nightmare as our already ragged emotions were being whipped around the roller coaster one more time. "If I have to be the one to make the decision to pull the plug, I can't do that," I told the lawyer.

Voicing the horrible reality of what might lay ahead broke the dam of emotions that had been building inside over the last several hours. As the pent-up tears poured down my cheeks, it actually began a healing effect as it released the fear that had been gripping my heart. In its place a steely resolve began to take over. Instead of giving up, I felt a renewed strength to fight for our baby. I knew immediately what needed to be done.

"While I appreciate your explanation of the situation, I need to speak to the doctor," I stated firmly. We finally got that chance nine hours later.

As we talked with the doctors, we wanted to know the extent of the complicated birth and the chances for survival. "It's just too soon to tell," they told us, noncommittal in their response. "If he lives, he may not walk until he is two or talk until he is five." We just don't know. We have to get him stabilized first, and then we can start running tests."

After gleaning as much information as possible from the doctors, we were finally able to see the baby. From his body ran numerous tubes connecting him to the machines that kept him alive. The moment we saw him, our decision was made. This was our son. This was the child God had promised to us, and no matter how bleak things appeared, we knew it was going to be okay. "We love you, Mitchell. You're going to make it," we spoke to him, touching his swollen body as we continued to pray.

Although doctors had projected a long hospital stay, slow recovery, and delayed development, Mitchell surprised them all. Within five days, his organs began working on their own, and he was removed from life support. Additional tests, which had previously shown irregular brain waves, now showed no abnormality as doctors and nurses alike commented at Mitchell's miraculous turnaround. Comparing the current test results to the previous tests, several of the medical staff commented, "This is so odd."

"No, this is God!" was our reply.

Five days after Mitchell was disconnected from the ventilator, we were finally able to take him home. The ten-day hospital ordeal, in which we had nearly lost him, was finally over. Mitchell and his birth mother had both made a complete and miraculous recovery.

It was a beautiful spring day in May as we walked out of the hospital almost four years ago, holding our miracle baby. Fifteen years we had waited for this child, but God's timing was perfect as we embraced our miracle baby. It was Mother's Day.

As of this writing, Mitchell is about to celebrate his fourth birthday. He is now in K-4 and loves adventure, riding his bike, and playing with trucks, cars, and trains. He is not afraid of anything. He is completely normal in his physical, mental, and emotional development and loves His Creator and healer, Jesus. Mitchell truly is a walking miracle.

Dear God, I cry to You in my distress and pain. It seems so unfair to have a desire for children that I seemingly can never bear. Lord, You created me and You gave me this desire. I bring it to You. Fill me with Your peace. Heal my heart and my body as I cast these cares upon You. Amen.

WOMEN OF THE BIBLE

Hannah[23]

*"As surely as you live, my lord, I am the woman who
stood here beside you praying to the LORD. I prayed
for this child, and the LORD has granted me what
I asked of him. So now I give him to the LORD.
For his whole life he will be given over to the LORD."*

1 SAMUEL 1:26–28

Infertility has been increasing in almost epidemic propor-
tions in recent years. For every four couples who are able to
conceive effortlessly, there is one couple who will face an uphill
battle of questions, struggles, pain, and testing. Only those who
have been there can understand the pain and emotional roller
coaster as each month brings both fresh expectation and too
often disappointment.

Hannah is just one of several biblical women who faced this
challenge. It says in First Samuel 1:10 that, "in bitterness of soul
Hannah wept much and prayed to the LORD." And it could have
ended right there. But Hannah refused to give up. Although she
had the devoted love of her husband for her, it was not enough.
Hannah prayed to the Lord in her great anguish and grief. She
wanted a child and kept pressing on, fervent in prayerful
requests to the Lord.

---

[23] See 1 Samuel 1:1–20.

How many times had she been to the temple prior to this event, petitioning the Lord? How many heartfelt prayers had escaped her lips, hoping for a change in what seemed to be a permanent situation? It would have been easy and understandable had she given up.

But finally something changed. One year as Hannah again came before the Lord, the priest Eli noticed her. Belatedly realizing her fervent petition to the Lord, he prayed over her and blessed her, sending her away with the promise that God would grant her request.

And Hannah believed.

Would anything have changed had Hannah not believed Eli? What if she had left skeptically thinking, *I'll believe it when I see it?*

But she didn't. Hannah was "expectant" with a miracle from that moment. Immediately upon receiving the priest's blessing and prophetic word, her demeanor changed, and she went to eat. She was no longer fasting, but rejoicing, confident that her prayers were heard. Hannah became "expectant" spiritually, long before anything changed physically.

Infertility is just one of numerous battles we may face in which there are no pat answers and no quick fixes in this natural world. But "Jesus Christ is the same yesterday and today and forever" (Heb. 13:8), and He is not limited to the resources of this earth.

What He did for Hannah, He will do for you.

That doesn't mean your answer will come in the exact same way. But it will come if you don't give up.

Psalm 113:9 says, "He settles the barren woman in her home as a happy mother of children." So take your *discouragement* and receive *encouragement* as Hannah did. Your miracle may come through medical intervention, adoption, or natural conception. But it will come, so don't give up!

Dear God, Your Word says that children are a blessing from You, a reward. I choose today to walk by faith and continue to believe for the children that You have already birthed in my heart. And like Hannah, I will dedicate my children to You. Amen.

LIFE LESSONS

1. Don't be bitter at God; take the bitterness to God.
2. Don't give up. What He will do for one, He will do for you.
3. Faith acts as if it has the miracle now, so rejoice!

DIVORCE

Kay Arthur[24]

I waited patiently for the LORD; he turned to me
and heard my cry. He lifted me out of the slimy pit,
out of the mud and mire; he set my feet on a rock
and gave me a firm place to stand. He put a new
song in my mouth, a hymn of praise to our God.
Many will see and fear and put their trust in the LORD.

PSALM 40:1–3

My platinum wedding band rolled round and round on the
rec room floor, making a mockery of what was taking place.
Tom was on the floor, groping, looking for my diamond engagement ring in the shadows of the table lamps. As I stood in the
corner of the room, looking on the scene like a detached specta-
tor, my lips were taut. No crying. No more hysterical sobbing. I
was beyond that. As far as I was concerned, it was over.

The wedding band had finally stopped spinning in circles. It lay dormant—just like our marriage. Tom was still looking for the engagement ring. I had thrown it at him along with my wedding band. He was murmuring something about how expensive the ring was. That made me sick!

I thought, *You care more about that stupid, expensive diamond ring than you do about me! Don't you know what has happened? I have taken off my wedding band! The one you have engraved with the words, 'Our Love Is Eternal.' Don't you realize—hasn't it occurred to you, Tom Goetz—that it has never been off my hand since the day of our wedding?*

The quarrel had begun in our bedroom. I didn't want to go back, so I stayed downstairs. For the first time in our six years of marriage, Tom had slapped me. I'd cut him down with my tongue. It was too much for him. He just couldn't handle it. He lost control. As the warm, salty blood from my nose touched my lips, I told Tom it was over—finished. He had followed me downstairs, pleading. Now he went to bed, alone.

Whether Tom slept or not, I don't know. I only know that the next day we called our priest. It was cut and dried. He thought we ought to separate. I would take our young sons, Tom and Mark, and move back to Arlington, Virginia, where I had friends. It was that simple—on the outside. Inside an unseen but very real wound began to fester. Its poison slowly began seeping into my soul. If the wound had been mine alone, it wouldn't have been nearly as bad. I didn't know how badly the boys were hurting—they never cried in front of me.

I never thought I would go through a divorce. There had always been only one thing I ever wanted in life, and that was to be happily married forever and ever—just like my mom and dad.

I wanted to be wildly in love—just like in the movies. I wanted an all-American husband who loved his wife and children. I wanted us all to live happily ever after. I would have been content to stay at home, to be the wife of a successful businessman. To raise my all-American boys, to dance away the weekends in the arms of my husband, laughing and enjoying the company of our friends.

Now after six years of marriage, the dream was over. My dream had become a nightmare. And it hurt. I had failed. The one and only thing I had ever wanted—to be happily married to one man until death parted us at an old age—was over. It had come and gone. I was only twenty-six years old.

Oh, it hurt! But not as badly as it was going to! I was so self-centered, so bent on my own happiness that I never really comprehended how badly it had hurt Tom. He didn't want a divorce. We just followed bad advice given by someone in a clerical collar. Once we were separated, the divorce seemed to follow naturally.

Tom hated living alone. He would call me and tell me that he was going to a psychiatrist. When I asked why, he said that he couldn't forget the awful things I had said to him.

From time to time when we talked, he would tell me that he was going to commit suicide. Thinking I would bluff him out of it, I would say, "Go ahead. But do a good job so I get your money!" His hurt became a wound—a wound that would go deeper with every phone call, every letter. Deeper until he put a rope around his neck. He died, his hurt never healed. Never able to hear my cry of "I'm sorry! If only I had known."

For me, it would be different. One day I would cry out, "Heal me, O Lord, and I will be healed! Save me, O Lord, and I will be saved!" I would discover that there was a balm in Gilead that could heal the sin-sick soul. How I wish I could have shared what I learned with Tom!

I have a message for you, beloved reader. One of hope, of life, of peace. Not my message, not psychology's, but God's! Whatever your wound, your hurt—whether it is mostly a self-inflicted wound like mine or whether it is a wound inflicted by others—God's Word says that there is a balm in Gilead, that there is a Great Physician there. And because that is true, you can cry out, "Heal me, O LORD, and I will be healed; save me and I will be saved, for Thou art my praise" (Jer. 17:14).

I believe any child of God can be healed of the deepest, most horrendous wounds if he will learn three things: how to apply the balm of Gilead, how to follow the Great Physician's instructions, and how to give His medicine time to work.

All of my hurt—living with Tom's suicide, coping with the memories of failing my two sons by divorcing their father and exposing them to my ensuing immorality—would be healed by this same balm and by my Great Physician whom I would come to know as Abba Father.

Dear God, divorce has left such ugly wounds—on me, my husband, and my children. Even our friends are affected. I need the balm of Gilead. Pour it into our wounds. Heal and forgive me. Show me where to go from here. Amen.

KAY ARTHUR is one of America's best known and most-beloved Bible teachers and authors. With her husband, Jack, she is the cofounder of Precept Ministries International, the leaders in inductive Bible-study resources. Kay also reaches hundreds of thousands of people internationally through her *Precept upon Precept* inductive Bible studies. In addition, she is known globally through her daily and weekly television and radio programs.

LIVING IN A CAVE

Cindy

"Forget the former things; do not dwell on the past.
See, I am doing a new thing! Now it springs up;
do you not perceive it? I am making a way
in the desert and streams in the wasteland."

ISAIAH 43:18–19

I sat in front of the mirror the night before the wedding and stared at my reflection. Instead of joyous feelings of anticipation, my heart was filled with dread as I thought of the upcoming ceremony.

I'm about to make the biggest mistake of my life.

In everyone's eyes, Gary and I made the perfect couple. Both of us Christians, we appeared very successful outwardly, and everyone thought we were inwardly. Gary had served as president of the youth group while I had been chaplain of my junior class. Over the past few years, we had both been actively involved in ministry and had a desire to continue after marriage. It seemed like a great match destined for great things.

But weeks prior to the wedding, I began to notice the dents in the armor of my "knight" as his melancholy moods brought outbursts of anger and depression. Growing up, my mother had experienced two nervous breakdowns and twenty-one shock treatments. Because of her constant mood swings, I remember my childhood as both difficult and fearful, never knowing what to expect when I walked in the door. Would she be in a good mood, or would she throw something at me? I was horrified when I finally realized the similarities between my mother and my fiancé.

In spite of my misgivings, I continued in the relationship. Contrary to our Christian upbringing, we had already become sexually intimate with one another. Because I knew in God's eyes we were already one, I felt I had no choice but to remain in the relationship. But neither of us was ready for the commitment of marriage.

Gary's depression and anger were rooted in his past. His father's harsh and uncaring attitude left him feeling unloved and insignificant. He vowed from an early age that once he grew up, he would be both successful and married to a wife who would compensate for all the love he hadn't received as a child. He was determined that he would never feel unloved again. But his unrealistic expectations of marriage were not the only unhealthy aspect of our relationship.

I came into the relationship with multiple medical problems and a history of more than thirty surgeries. Not only was my

health fragile, but my emotional stability was worse. Because of
my constant need for medical attention due to a condition I'd had
from birth, my mother had told me that I was the reason for her
nervous breakdowns and suicidal thoughts. Subsequently, I grew
up believing that everyone would be better off without me, and I
emotionally crawled into a cave, hoping to find a sense of security that my home life did not provide. As long as I lived in my
cave, nobody could find me, and more importantly, nobody could
hurt me.

But then I married Gary.

Gary's intense psychological need for love and acceptance
forced me deeper into my cave and away from him. The deeper
I withdrew, the more heated the arguments became until our
home was a constant battleground.

In the midst of our marital difficulties, however, there was a
bright ray of hope. Doctors had told me I would never conceive,
but after three years of marriage, we held our miracle child. But
even Jenny's bright countenance could not heal our wounded
hearts as the arguments increased in intensity.

One evening after Jenny had gone to bed, the familiar
routine began. The noise of yelling and the thud of thrown
objects terrified our now ten-year-old daughter, who feared I
would be physically injured. The next morning she informed me
that her bags were packed.

"I'm going to the 7-11 and calling Grandma and Grandpa to
come and get me," she firmly stated. "We need to get away, Mom."

Her simple declaration finally brought me to a place of decision for her emotional health as well as my own. Because of my own self-hatred, I had actually embraced Gary's rages and in an odd sense felt better after his verbal lashings. It became a form of penance, which I felt I deserved. That day as Jenny stood resolutely before me, I could finally admit that I was just as emotionally sick as he. She and I left that day, and I later filed for divorce.

Now free from Gary, Jenny and I moved into a small garage apartment that my parents built especially for us. Mom's and my relationship had healed over the past eight years as had her emotional and physical health. For the next five years, this apartment became my safe haven where God could finally perform surgery on my wounded soul. I secluded myself in our small fortress as I battled my own insecurities. I finally had the "security" I had always desired in this small refuge, but I had no life and nothing to do.

You're nice and safe, I heard the Lord speak to me one day. *Are you happy now?*

In my mind I saw Him smiling down at me, loving me, having given me exactly what I had asked for. But I wasn't happy. For what is life without risk? And what is life without pain? My "perfect" world, I found, was less than perfect. As the Lord guided me to trust Him with my life, my daughter, and every other area, He gently drew me out of my cave. Without my even realizing it, the fortress walls I had erected around my life began to crumble.

Immediately after the divorce, God had begun surgery on Gary's heart, taking him halfway around the world to complete the task. For the next few years, Gary dedicated his life to missions. Having lost his wife and daughter, and away from all he once held dear, God had him right in the palm of His hand. As He worked through the painful areas of Gary's life, He confronted him with his idolatry—that of looking to me and our daughter to provide him the love and significance that could only come from God.

It was a slow work, but while Gary left America a wounded and broken individual, now five years after the divorce as he relocated back to the States, he was changed, completely surrendered to the Lord. "If I never have love. If I do nothing more in my life than pass out bulletins on Sunday morning," Gary finally conceded to the Lord, "Your love is enough."

With that declaration, the final walls in Gary's life crumbled as well. In the midst of the ruin, God could now rebuild a miraculous union.

It was a warm Sunday morning in August as I joined the other members of the choir. Ironically, the song that morning was about walls coming down. As the Spirit of God fell on our church, I knelt before the Lord. Tears streamed down my face as His presence filled the room. "What is going on?" I prayed.

Watch and see what I am going to do, God responded in my heart. I felt like Moses standing at the Red Sea just before the Lord was about to part the water. There was such anticipation in my spirit.

Little did I know that in another area of town where Gary attended church, their congregation was experiencing a similar move of the Lord. Similarly, Gary fell on his face and prayed, "Lord, what do You want me to do?"

But unlike the deeply spiritual message he might have expected, he received a simple instruction: *Go buy a car.*

After returning to the States, Gary had been given an old, beat-up vehicle for transportation. It got him where he needed to go, but had been a great source of embarrassment to Jenny. In obedience, directly after church Gary went to a car lot and purchased a sleek, black, older model Acura. He immediately drove it over to show it to Jenny.

"Jenny isn't here," my mother told Gary in response to his knock at the door. "But I'll get Cindy."

Gary and I had maintained a civil relationship since his return. So when he asked me if I wanted to go for a quick ride, I accepted. The waters were about to part.

As Gary pulled out of the driveway and we began to talk, it was immediately evident to me that something was different. Just like the words of the song from the morning service, the walls were coming down between us. When Gary pulled back into the driveway, I invited him inside, and we continued to talk. Before he left that evening, we knew that God was mending our relationship. But he had to convince my family first.

The next morning as I went to work with my mom, I brought up the subject. "Mom, I know that you and Dad are not very excited about the prospect of Gary and me getting back together, but all I can tell you is God is doing something."

Mom smiled as she revealed her own secret.

"Honey, several months ago your dad and I were talking about you, concerned for your future. Later that night God woke me up and told me, *Don't worry about Cindy. I have saved her for her husband and will bring them back together.*

"I already knew this day would come," she explained knowingly.

My dad was not so easily convinced. About six weeks after Gary and I had started seeing each other, my dad walked into the room and said with a trembling voice, "I'm ready to talk with Gary."

When Gary arrived, he followed Dad into the back room where they shut the door. It was a moment of truth. Skeptically Dad began the inquisition, "How have you changed and why?"

Four hours later when they emerged from that small room, another miracle occurred as Dad spoke to Gary, "If you and Cindy decide to remarry, you have my blessing."

All that remained now was Jenny.

Now sixteen years old, Jenny was unflinching. "Mom, I'm happy for you and Dad, but I don't want him back. Can't you wait until I move off to college?" she pleaded.

I understood her pain, but I understood more importantly that without healing in their relationship, Jenny would never experience a healthy relationship with any man.

"Opening my heart to Dad feels like I am jumping off a cliff," she tearfully confessed a few days later as the subject came up again. "I don't know if I am going to be dashed to pieces or if someone is going to catch me."

"Jenny, the only way you are going to find out is to jump," I replied, certain of the outcome. Not long after, Jenny was ready, and in her mind she jumped—and saw the Lord catch her. Her relationship with Gary did not change overnight. In fact, it took almost three years for God to completely heal the pain of the past, but He did.

Gary and I remarried on June fifth, ten years ago. God restored our marriage, our family, and our ministry. In our pain God revealed Himself to us. He took us past our head knowledge of Him and walked with us, even in our brokenness, and let us experience His great love and healing so that now we can say we truly know Him and deeply love each other.

Dear God, You are a miracle worker. You know the pain of broken relationships, because Your relationship with all mankind was broken because of our sin. But You healed our relationship with You through Jesus, and I'm asking You to heal the broken relationships in my life. Amen.

THE HEALING
OF A
WOUNDED HEART

$\mathcal{N}$orma

*I lift up my eyes to the hills—where does my
help come from? My help comes from the LORD,
the Maker of heaven and earth.*

PSALM 121:1–2

You take one broken, wounded person, and he or she
marries another broken, wounded person, and the two don't
make a whole. They make a mess.

I didn't come from a warm home. Instead, I came from a
broken one with a mother and stepfather who were emotionally
absent. I was never abused physically, but if you call withhold-
ing love abuse, then I was abused. I was raised in the era that
when women graduated from high school, they got married and
had babies. If a girl didn't have a boyfriend, she was nothing. So
when I met Clifford when I was seventeen, he gave me the
attention and social status I needed.

But the years of rejection I had experienced as a child had taken their toll as my insecurity and lack of confidence influenced every area of my life. I was nineteen years old when, after one year of college, I convinced myself that I would fail. Nobody else in my family had made it through college. How could I? Looking back, I think if just one person had encouraged me to continue, I might have stayed on course. Instead, I got married.

It was just a few years into my marriage that I realized I was in trouble as a distinct personality change came over my husband. Never a compassionate and loving individual, my husband now became cruel and calloused as the abuse he had received as a child began to surface in him. But nobody but the two of us knew. Nobody.

I remember one day a woman from church commented, "Norma, you are so lucky. Your husband just adores you."

On the outside we appeared to be the perfect couple. But in reality, we lived a nightmare of cruel verbal abuse and fear. I was so ashamed of what was happening in my home that I wouldn't tell a soul.

I never wanted to become a statistic. My mother had divorced as had my two uncles and my sister. It was not where I wanted to go, so for twenty-three years I stayed in my marriage. But each day our situation became more difficult. While the last ten years were really hard, the final four were terrifying as his verbal abuse escalated to the point where my children and I feared for our lives. Eventually I had to flee with my two kids—my son then in college, my daughter a junior in high school.

I wish I could say we divorced because we didn't know God. While this would have been true had we divorced at the beginning of our marriage, it couldn't be our excuse at the end, as somewhere in between we had accepted God into our lives. The real reason for the divorce was that we were two broken people. I allowed his behavior, becoming an enabler as I covered up for him in my embarrassment. When I finally did attempt to make a stand, it was too late as he had become a seething caul-dron of anger toward us.

After the divorce, although we no longer feared for our lives, I was now faced with the daunting responsibility of pro-viding for myself and my two children alone. The rebuilding process was long and slow. Over the past seventeen years since the divorce, God has mercifully sent people and information into my life to help guide me through the long healing process.

From the beginning, interestingly, I wasn't afraid to be alone, but allowed God to shine His light on the hurt and wounded places of my life. I've learned that when we are afraid to be alone, it is often because we are afraid of what we will find at the core. True healing can only come when we allow God into the deepest recesses of our lives.

One precious lady in my church approached me recently and said, "Well, I know you must get lonely at times."

"Let me stop you right there," I interjected. "I don't."

"Really?" she exclaimed in disbelief.

"Really," I said.

And that is part of the tremendous work God has done in my life. He has so filled my life that I am never lonely. I have learned to embrace solitude with no TV, no radio, and no noise. Solitude can be a friend if you are friends with yourself and with the Lord.

Today I am a published author, I teach Sunday school, and I travel across the nation speaking at writers' conferences. Thanks to God's work in my life, I know whose I am and where I am going. These are victories I could have never achieved had I not walked in forgiveness and allowed God time to heal my wounded heart. I could look back and say, "That man destroyed twenty-three years of my life!" Instead, I choose to say, "Look where God is taking me."

Dear God, only You know how I got to this place. I feel like a worthless failure who has no hope for a decent life. But in my heart, I know You are my hope and that You can work miracles. I give You my life, just as I am, and ask You to make something of it. Thank You for loving me. Help me love myself. Amen.

WOMEN OF THE BIBLE
Abigail[25]

For you who revere my name, the sun of righteousness
will rise with healing in its wings. And you will go
out and leap like calves released from the stall.

MALACHI 4:2

Abigail found herself married to a wealthy man who was
known as "surly and mean in his dealings" and "such a wicked
man that no one [could] talk to him" (1 Sam. 25:3,17). But in spite
of a failing marriage and an uncommunicative and wicked
husband, we find that Abigail did not become bitter, feel sorry
for herself, or blame God. Instead, the Bible describes her as not
only beautiful, but also intelligent and prudent in the care of her
home and servants. Instead of cursing her wicked husband, she
interceded on his behalf, asking that he be forgiven. It was
because of this faithfulness and wisdom that after her husband's
death, she was chosen by David to be his wife.

LIFE LESSONS

1. If your marriage is failing or has already failed, take comfort
    in the fact Jesus has not forsaken you; you are not alone.

2. Do not allow bitterness, unforgiveness, or anger to fester in
    your heart. Instead, allow God to heal your hurts and wounds.

3. Remain faithful to God and keep your heart right, so He can
    bring restoration to you. God's good plan for you has not
    changed, and He can get you back on track.

---

[25] See 1 Samuel 25:1–42.

IT'S WORSE
THAN WE
THOUGHT

Doni Crouch

The LORD sustains them on their sickbed;
in their illness you heal all their infirmities.

PSALM 41:3 NRSV

The surgeon walked out to the waiting area where my
husband, Van, and my daughter waited for news of the surgery
that was to remove two cancerous tumors from my liver. The
surgery was supposed to take three hours. It had been less than
an hour when the surgeon neared, causing Van to wonder
briefly how the surgery could have been completed so soon.

"Things are worse than we thought," the doctor began.
"Instead of two tumors, your wife has five. At this point you
have three choices," he stated as he outlined our options. None
of the choices was encouraging. At best he gave me a 50/50
chance of surviving the surgery.

"We're praying for you and for the surgery," Van reminded him as the surgeon returned to the operating room. It would be a long day.

I had begun experiencing flu-like symptoms that occurred with common regularity eight years before. After numerous tests, doctors were unable to detect any major problems until a serious back injury sent me to a chiropractor. The adjustment went seriously wrong. Three swift yanks left me bedridden for six months with three months of therapy and steroids. The back pain and subsequent steroid use masked the more serious problem that had been lurking in my body for the past several years, allowing its continued growth.

When it was finally discovered, I had third stage colon cancer, which had spread to my lymph system and liver. There are only two additional stages of progression with the disease, the fifth stage, Heaven.

The surgeon returned to the waiting room with a smile eight hours later. "Once I got back in the operating room, I figured out an additional option. We were able to completely remove three of the five tumors and resection the remaining part. This was the best we could hope for," he concluded. It was just one of many miracles in the long walk ahead.

Although the surgeon had completed his difficult task, the hard work was just beginning for me as I began the slow recovery from this painful surgery and the chemotherapy, which continued for the next two and a half months.

"Are you willing to fight this?" Van asked at the beginning, knowing the battle that still lay ahead.

"Yes, if you won't let the ministry die," I countered. My husband is an evangelist and motivational speaker, which requires constant travel. It didn't seem possible for him to continue his work and take care of me at the same time. Our home church, recognizing our dilemma, helped set up a group of caregivers who took turns staying with me during the weekends, so Van could continue to minister. These dedicated women came into our home to cook, clean, and pray. Often I was too sick to even notice their presence, yet they remained, enabling us to continue through an impossible situation.

Each day I would spend at least four hours reading Scriptures on healing and listening to tapes of the same. When the pain became so severe that I could no longer read, I continued to meditate on the Word of God through audiotapes, taking communion often as a remembrance of our covenant promise of healing.

There were days I felt so weak that I couldn't talk or even lift my head off the pillow. On those days I told the Lord, "You know I love You, but today I'm just going to crawl up in Your arms and let You hold me because I can't do anything else."

We had to fight not only cancer, but fear. But God placed strategic individuals, doctors, surgeons, nurses, and friends along our path to stand with us during the difficult process. Their prayers could be felt and gave us strength to continue.

Once a week we went to the hospital for the chemotherapy. It was the only decent day I would have all week. Van and I would dress up for our special "date." The hospital staff had a great sense of humor as we bantered through the afternoon, as the clear liquid dripped into my system. By the time it was finished, we would have just enough time for a nice dinner and then church before the effects of the chemotherapy would begin racking my body with pain. There were times I felt so ice cold due to my decreased blood count that I thought, *This is what death must feel like.* I have sensed death near, but it can't have me.

I have since completed all chemotherapy treatments. Additional blood tests and a colonoscopy have all been free of cancer as the doctors continue to monitor my progress.

A good friend once said to me, "A quality decision eliminates temptation." From the beginning, we resolved to choose life and take God at His Word. With that decision, a new strength came alongside us to enable us to fight back with a strength that was not our own. I could never have fought this battle alone, and thankfully through this struggle we have been reminded that He will never require us to.

Dear God, thank You for reminding me that I am not alone in my battles, that You also fight for me. Strengthen me, infuse me with courage and determination, fill me with hope for the future and faith in Your Word. You always cause me to triumph in Christ, so that means we win![20] Amen.

DONI CROUCH is now considered medically cancer free and has been given a clean bill of health for the past two years. She and her husband, evangelist and motivational speaker Van Crouch, travel across the U. S. sharing a message of hope, humor, and enthusiasm. For more information call (630) 682-8300 or E-mail vancrouch@aol.com.

---

[20] See 2 Corinthians 2:14.

THERE IS
NO CURE

Pam

Worship the LORD your God, and his
blessing will be on your food and water.
I will take away sickness from among you.

EXODUS 23:25

"I have good news and bad news," the doctor said entering my room. "The good news is that we found out what is wrong with you. The bad news is there is no cure."

Shortly after my father died, I started getting sick. It began with pain that would shoot through my body, leaving me doubled over in pain, lasting for five to ten days. This was a cycle that would repeat itself over and over each month for the next four years. I was only twenty-five years old at the time with a husband and a five-month-old baby.

The bouts were severe, often requiring hospitalization for dehydration as I was unable to keep food or water down. But month after month after the completion of the five- to ten-day cycle, all symptoms would disappear as mysteriously as they

began. Exploratory surgery yielded no clues as to the mysterious ailment. "It's all in your head," I was told after several tests
produced no conclusive evidence. "Your father just passed away,
and the symptoms you are experiencing are psychosomatic." I
heard this so often that after a while even I began to believe it.
But the painful monthly cycle continued, forcing me to return
again and again to the doctor for more tests. Doctors finally
concluded that it must be female problems due to its monthly
consistency, yet medical tests were still inconclusive as to the
exact cause of this mysterious illness.

As the pattern continued, I had to completely reevaluate my
theology on healing and what I believed. My dad had just died of
complete respiratory failure from asthma. Raised in a Christian
home that believed in God's healing power, my father's death
and my own strange illness had shaken me to the core. My
father had believed for his healing and died. I knew of many
others who had believed God for healing in my past. Some had
been healed, while others had not. Was I going to be one that
was healed, or one that was not? What did I really believe?

I began in earnest to study the Scriptures for myself. As I
studied, it became apparent that in the Bible everyone who came
to Jesus to be healed went away healed. My husband remem-
bers the day I walked in and told him, "I am going
to believe God for my healing, and I'm not
going to settle for anything less!" I had come
to a crossroads and chosen the path of
God's healing. I was determined to believe
God for my miracle.

But the path I had chosen was not an easy one.

My husband, Jim, is an evangelist. At that time in our lives, we were traveling all over the United States preaching in different churches. It seemed that during my illness, Jim began to teach increasingly on healing.

"Jimmy, you have got to quit preaching healing," I told him after several months. "Here I am sick, everyone knows I'm sick, and you are teaching on healing. We must be a laughingstock everywhere we go."

I remember my husband's words distinctly: "Pam, I will never quit preaching healing, because it is the Word of God."

It was a step of faith for us. So I continued to study the Scriptures on healing and kept my mouth shut to any words contrary to what God had said, determined to find God's answer.

As we would minister in churches, I would be in so much pain that I could barely sit through the services. As the meetings would get underway, Jim would call me to the front to sing. It took effort just walking to the platform, each step filled with pain until I opened my mouth to sing praise to God. That is when I began to notice a pattern. Every time I sang, the pain would stop and would not return until I finished singing and returned to my seat.

Another instance confirmed this revelation. One evening when Jim was out ministering, my mother had come to stay with me. In the middle of the night, the pain was so intense that I was literally rolling around on the floor curled up in a ball.

My mother felt helpless as she stood in the room praying, unable to ease my pain. Suddenly she stopped praying and began to sing. Instantly the pain left. Eventually, though, she grew tired and quit. Immediately the pain returned. "Momma, you have to keep singing," I pleaded. As she resumed, the pain disappeared. The power of praise was driving the pain from my body.

As time and the illness progressed, the doctors remained baffled. Finally, my local doctors sent me to the City of Faith Hospital in Tulsa, Oklahoma, which was still in operation at the time. This was the hospital built by Oral Roberts to be an institution that combined the power of prayer with medicine. They ran a battery of tests until one morning Dr. Don King came into my room and said, "I have good news and bad news. The good news is that we have found out what is wrong with you. The bad news is there is no cure." My illness was called "Familiar Mediterranean Fever"—a rare blood disorder that can occur in people of Mediterranean decent. My Italian heritage made me a candidate.

Hearing the bleak diagnosis did not cause the devastation you might think, however. In fact, I wasn't upset at all. The months of studying the biblical Scriptures on healing had strengthened my faith and resolve to stand for my healing, despite what the doctors might say or what my body might feel. For Jim and me, the issue was already settled in our minds regarding my healing. Now we simply had a name for the battle we were facing.

While at the City of Faith, we had asked the staff if the Roberts family ever visited the hospital. They informed us that due to their busy schedules, Oral and his wife, Evelyn, did not. We did receive a visit from their daughter, Roberta, one day, and we enjoyed our brief conversation with her. It was a few days later that the doctors performed a liver biopsy to test for something in regard to the disease. I was still a little woozy from the medication they had given me for the procedure when Jim came into my room and said, "Oral Roberts is outside and is about to come into your room in case you want to fix your hair."

"Right," I said in disbelief. My husband loves to play tricks on me, and I was certain this was one of those times. However, a few minutes later the nurse came in with the same message, "Oral Roberts is just outside and will be in momentarily." Now I was scrambling to locate my brush and mirror!

As Brother Roberts entered the room, he walked straight to the bed and took my hand, saying, "I want you to repeat after me. 'In the name of Jesus, I am being healed.'" After he prayed, he shook Jim's hand and turned to leave. But as he reached the door, he turned back and said, "That's what He told me to tell you today."

The presence of the Lord had filled the room. After Oral left, I looked at Jim and said, "What do you think?"

"There is no doubt about it; the man has the gift of healing," he replied. The power of God was so thick in the air that you could have cut it with a knife.

I can pinpoint the beginning of my healing to that day as the monthly cycles of pain stopped their regularity, but the battle wasn't over yet. As I reflected on Brother Roberts' visit, I thought it was interesting that the words he had me repeat in prayer were, "In the name of Jesus, I am being healed." *Being* healed. My healing was not an instantaneous miracle, but a process that took place over the next few months.

During that time, I experienced two more bouts of the illness that were extremely severe. It was during this time that another scripture had been introduced to us from Exodus 23:25 NKJV: "He will bless your bread and water. And I will take sickness away from the midst of you." As that scripture became clear to our hearts Jim, as spiritual head of our home, began to pray over our home as never before.

When the pain returned the last time with such severity—I was again unable to keep any food or water down—Jim knew that if it continued, I would have to go back into the hospital. An anger and hatred for the sickness and Satan rose up so strongly that he went through the house praying and demanding Satan to get out. He began to speak God's Word over our home, our family, and everything in it. He then went to the kitchen cabinet and pulled out a can of chicken noodle soup, poured it into a bowl, and heated it in the microwave. As he did, he prayed that every noodle, all the broth, and every piece of chicken would be blessed according to Exodus 23:25 and declared that God was removing sickness from our midst. He then brought the warmed bowl of soup to my room for me to eat.

Up to that time, I had been unable to keep any food or liquid down, and greasy chicken soup was the last thing I wanted. But Jim encouraged me to eat and continued to pray as I lifted the spoon to my lips. Not only was I able to eat the entire bowl of soup and keep it down, but the battle had been won. I never had another reoccurrence of the painful cycles that had plagued me for four long years. That was eighteen years ago!

If you are battling illness today, don't give up. The Bible encourages us to "fight the good fight of faith" (1 Tim. 6:12 NKJV). It is a fight. It isn't easy. I think one of the reasons that some people aren't healed is that they give up too soon. There are times I wanted to give up. I even wanted to kill myself as I heard Satan say to me, *You're going to die anyway, so just get it over with. Your husband is tired of having a sick wife and you are no good to your children.* It would have been easier to give up. Every time I went to stand in a healing line, he would taunt me, *People are sick of praying for you, why don't you just sit down?* The thought was tempting.

Another battle you must overcome is the one of your own mind. Too often we allow someone else's life experience to determine the outcome for our lives. For example, "Grandma was believing for her healing and she died," or "My friend had asked for prayer and she died."

Romans 3:3 encourages us not to let someone else's unbelief make the Word of God of no effect in our life. That is not to say that just because someone else didn't get healed they didn't have faith, but we have to forget what happened in their life and focus on what God has said in His Word. What are you going to believe? The physical symptoms? Or the truth of healing from the Word of God? I encourage you to do as the Bible says: "Choose life, so that you and your children may live" (Deut. 30:19).

Dear God, I choose to worship You no matter what the circumstances look like or feel like. I choose to believe Your Word regarding healing and say, "By Jesus' stripes, I am healed." I walk by faith and not by what I see, hear, or feel. All fear must go because God's love drives out fear, and He has not given me a spirit of fear but of power, love, and a sound mind. Amen.[27]

---

[27] See 1 Peter 2:24; 2 Corinthians 5:7; 1 John 4:18; and 2 Timothy 1:7.

HEALING CAN
BE A PROCESS

Michelle

*Praise the LORD, O my soul, and forget not
all His benefits—who forgives all your
sins and heals all your diseases.*

PSALM 103:2-3

I was sitting at my desk attempting to read the information on the blue screen of my PC monitor. I rubbed my eyes again, willing the figures to come back into focus. With deadlines looming, I didn't have time for any delays. *Why can't I read the figures on the screen just inches in front of me?* I had experienced similar symptoms a few years before—blurred vision and occasional double vision. "It's stress related," the doctor confirmed after a checkup. "Just try to keep things calmer, and you should do fine," he encouraged.

But the symptoms kept reoccurring, and things weren't fine at all. I returned to the doctor, and he performed a MRI and several other tests to determine the cause of the disturbing symptoms. When I met with him later for the test results, he gave me his surprising report.

"We're not sure, but we think you might have multiple sclerosis (MS)," he said.

I was devastated, but in denial in many respects. After all, the doctor said they didn't know for sure. Maybe they were wrong. But in spite of my own hopeful reassurances, my mind kept returning to a friend who had been diagnosed with MS a few years earlier. Eventually she had to go on permanent disability because the disease had severely affected her speech and ability to walk.

That won't happen to me, I thought to myself. But I was wrong.

The symptoms gradually disappeared, and life returned to the normal routine of high stress and long work hours until a family crisis once again shook the fragile condition of my health. I received word that my mother had suffered a major stroke. I was very upset, and the increased stress from this incident triggered the MS symptoms once more. Only this time they didn't go away.

My health gradually worsened due to the continuous stress, and eventually I was forced to leave my job. With no job, my self-esteem plummeted to an all-time low. I felt like a failure. I felt like I had no responsibility, and therefore I had no purpose. But in the midst of these negative circumstances, I knew I was valuable to God.

In reality I had so much to be thankful for. I had a wonderful, loving husband and key friends who stood with me in prayer for my healing. During this time, I read about an athlete who had been diagnosed with MS. He made the statement, "Doctors may say that I have MS, but MS is not going to have me!"

I took hold of that word. I had a choice to make. I could focus on the doctor's diagnosis, or I could focus on the Word of God. I chose the latter. I have also chosen to make nutritional changes by improving my eating habits and including nutritional supplements in my diet. I believe many people make the mistake of praying for their healing while at the same time abusing their bodies with poor eating habits. It won't work. I have made changes to my diet—not only my nutritional diet, but my spiritual diet as well—and I have seen dramatic results!

Two years ago at my annual checkup, my physician ended the session by saying, "You're about the same." But then she paused a moment and said, "Actually, you're improving."

All I could say was "glory to God!"

Although I still face challenges with MS symptoms, these symptoms only cause me to press closer to God and His Word that says, "By His stripes, [I am] healed" (Isa. 53:5 NKJV).

It's been sixteen years since I received that fateful diagnosis. I am not in a wheelchair, nor am I experiencing daily symptoms. It has been a slow progression towards the ultimate goal of total health, but I have grown much closer to God during this process. While I am not where I want to be physically, I also am not where I was either. An instantaneous healing would be wonderful. But in the meantime, I will continue to trust in God and fulfill the purpose and plan that He has for my life.

Dear God, help me keep my eyes on You and not on how I feel. It's difficult to pray when my body is filled with pain and when I see the symptoms of my illness before me each day. But I will stay in an attitude of continually receiving Your healing power that drives sickness from my body. Give me strength to stand—no matter how long it takes—until I am completely whole. Amen.

WOMEN OF THE BIBLE

THE WOMAN WITH THE
ISSUE OF BLOOD[28]

*Faith comes from hearing what is told and that
hearing comes through the message about Christ.*

ROMANS 10:17 GSPD

Numerous healings are recorded throughout the Bible as
those in need reached out for a touch from God. Stop a minute
and ponder that fact. The Bible is *filled* with stories of individuals who stepped out of the crowd or outside the accepted
protocol to obtain their miracle. Lepers were healed, blind eyes
opened, the dead were raised. One notable miracle was that of
the woman who had been subject to bleeding for twelve years.
Having tried every doctor and all available medicine, instead of
getting better, she actually got worse and was now broke.
Medically there was no hope.

"If I but touch his clothes, I will be made well," (Mark 5:28
NRSV) she said to herself of Jesus. After years of discouragement, it is no small miracle that she could even muster the strength to
hope again. As the crowds pressed around Jesus that day, one
small woman pressed through in faith to simply touch Him.
Many must have brushed against Him in the crowd with no significance. However, as this woman reached out to obtain her
healing by faith, the ever-present healing power flowed out of

---

[28] See Mark 5:25–34.

235

Jesus into her. Jesus' response? "Daughter, your faith has made you well; go in peace, and be healed of your disease" (v. 34).

No matter what report the doctor may have given you, it doesn't change the fact that Jesus is the healer. You, too, can push past the crowd and the obstacles in your way to reach out and touch the hem of His garment. His healing power is still available today.

Dear God, I believe the same healing power that was available in the Bible is available to me today. I receive Your healing virtue and thank You that it is working a healing and a cure in my body. Thank You for sending Jesus to bear my sickness and pain on the cross. Amen.

LIFE'S LESSON

1. What is your need today? Press through the obstacles of doubt and fear to take hold of His ever-present promises for you.

2. Your faith is an active ingredient in the healing process that can increase as you hear the Word of God.

3. Don't give up. Don't buy into the lie that God gains glory by your sickness. John 10:10 says, "The thief comes only to steal and kill and destroy; I have come that they may have life, and have it to the full."

ABOUT CHINA

Thank you for purchasing *Seasons of Life*. By purchasing this book, you are also contributing to the ongoing ministry outreach to the people of China. The numerous Christian artists, authors, and ministers featured have graciously contributed their stories to assist in this fund-raising effort.

Although China is closed to the Gospel due to communism, God is opening doors of opportunity. Here are some recent statistics regarding China:

- 23,000 people die in China every day, most having never heard the Gospel of Jesus Christ.
- Suicide is the leading cause of death among Chinese women between the ages of 20 and 34.
- There is only approximately one Bible for every 100–200 Christians in rural parts of the country.
- Although the number of China's house churches is now conservatively estimated at 80 million, and growing all the time, it still represents less than 1 percent of the entire population.

The following story is true. We hope it will give you a glimpse into this nation, still needing to be reached with the Gospel of Jesus Christ.

THE BIKE RIDE

*He [Jesus] said to them, "Go into all the world
and preach the good news to all creation."*

MARK 16:15

It was a cloudy afternoon as I climbed onto the black,
single-speed, nondescript bicycle—the kind so typical in China.
Bundled in four layers of clothing to protect against the frigid
winter temperature, I readjusted my hat and gloves before ped-
aling through the neighborhood streets, eventually turning onto
the main road. Although the temperature was well below freezing outside, I was soon perspiring as I pumped the bike up the
steep hill, one of two I faced on my journey to the secret house-
church meeting of Chinese believers. The main road had protected bike lanes with traffic so heavy, at times, that I could
reach over and touch the cyclist next to me on either side. One
fall, and, like dominoes, everyone would go down. I tried not to
think about it.

Each week I met with several believers. This group was
one of my favorites. All in their twenties and thirties, some had
been my students in the English classes I taught at the university. Each of these individuals held positions of leadership within
the house-church movement, although somewhat reluctantly.

To avoid detection, the location of our meeting would often
vary, as would our route to the particular homes. Times of
praise and worship were little more than whispers of melodic
voices; nevertheless, God's presence was evident. The atmosphere in these homes was always warm and loving, regardless
of the weather outdoors, in this case freezing.

Twenty minutes later, I arrived and climbed the three flights of stairs, knocking lightly. The door opened immediately, and I was ushered inside. Familiar faces and delicious smells of the meal we would soon share were enough to warm my frozen cheeks and fingers. The "girls" began talking excitedly, sharing with me the adventures of the week. Most were still single, although two had married recently, one expecting a baby the following year.

I took off my hat, coat, and gloves and washed my hands in preparation for another lesson in Chinese cooking. The next several minutes were a blur of chopping and stir-frying as we created several dishes using egg plant, green beans, potatoes, pork, garlic, ginger, and of course, rice.

After clearing the table from our finished meal, we then pulled out our Bibles and began the Bible study. Most often what I would teach in this meeting would be the same text they would use in their larger underground meetings later in the week. Switching from English to Chinese and back again, there was somehow always a grace to communicate the message in a way I believe they could all understand. In spite of the cultural differences, we had become close friends as we shared meals, the simple truths of the Bible, and the deeper feelings of our hearts.

Almost four hours after the time I had arrived, I stood to rebundle for the cold return ride, made worse due to the lack of daylight. I felt my way back down the concrete stairwell, completely void of light except for the occasional opening of another door in the stairwell, as others were coming and going as well. Thank goodness I only had three flights to go down.

Stumbling over parked bikes, cabbage urns, and miscellaneous debris, I finally made my way to the bottom. As I opened the door, the frigid air blasted against my face as I instinctively lowered my head and walked against the wind to where I had locked my bike. Already my fingers were so cold it was difficult to insert the key and turn the lock.

Back on my bike, I made my way home as quickly as my tired legs would allow. The traffic was much lighter due to the late hour, and I finally turned off the main street to the winding back road, which was the final leg of the trip to our home. The road, although paved at the beginning, turned into a rutted dirt road halfway to the campus where we lived. Street lights were a luxury even on main roads. Back roads, such as this, on moon-less nights could be extremely difficult to navigate. At least I was familiar with this one.

On this particular stretch, it wasn't surprising to share the road with a flock of geese, a large sow, or even a couple of goats. But tonight it was empty and silent except for the sound of my own bike as it rattled and clattered over each hump. *Only one more corner, through the gate, and up the stairs,* I thought to myself of the remainder of my journey, including the five flights of steps to our small apartment. I was tired from the afternoon excursion. *Stay focused,* I told myself.

It was just as I was turning the last corner that I felt my front tire drop down into a large hole. Striking hard, I tumbled from the bike. Cold and now bruised, I struggled to my feet to try to determine what had caused the accident. As my eyes focused, I could see a large mound of dirt, which had once been part of the road, piled high next to the gaping hole in which my bike had plunged. I'm not sure what the purpose of the pit was, as "street repair" seemed a foreign concept in our city, especially on these back alleys. Frustrated I began to grumble to myself, *In*

America, they would never allow such hazards to exist! I can't believe someone would leave such a huge hole in the middle of the road and not put up any lights or rope or anything to prevent an accident! Silly thoughts that were of little assistance. I had to get home.

I pulled my bike out of the pit and checked the tires to ensure they both still had air. Amazingly, they did. Sore, however, I opted to walk the bike the short remaining stretch, finally reaching the tall, chain-link-fenced gate to the school compound. Pushing open the small bike opening, a door inside the larger locked gate, I lifted my bike up and over the metal bar. My muscles groaned with the effort as I circled the path to our apartment building just ahead of me. Typically, I would carry the bike inside and lock it to one of the radiator coils near our apartment, five flights up. On a good evening, this was difficult at best. Tonight, impossible. I locked the bike outside—more susceptible to possible theft, but I was too tired to care. I prayed a quick prayer over it and began my ascent to the top floor and home.

Finally inside where it was warmer, I shed a couple of layers and began to rub my hands together to restore warmth and circulation. I reflected back over the afternoon, the long, cold bike ride, delicious meal, Bible study, shared friendship, and finally the accident.

No one said life in China would be easy. Day after day we faced constant challenges of cultural differences, language barriers, and open prejudice. I closed my eyes as I sipped a mug of hot tea, enjoying the moment of quiet. Yes, I was exhausted and still a little shaken from the accident. But I would make that same trek again next week, and the next, and the next after that. In spite of the difficulties, danger, and discomfort of life in a foreign country, it was really a very small sacrifice when compared to God's immeasurable grace to accomplish the task. Yes, we have a choice, but His command is clear: "Go ye into all the world." He leaves the choice to us—comfort, or obedience? I'm so glad when Jesus was faced with this decision in the Garden of Gethsemane two thousand years ago, He made a decision for you and me out of obedience rather than choosing His own personal comfort. How can we choose anything less?

You may not be called to actually go to a foreign country to share the Gospel, but as believers we are all called to make sure the "sent ones" get there to bring the Good News. Do you sense a tug at your heart, a desire to go and do the work? Or are you moved with compassion to help others go?

By purchasing this book, you have made it possible for our work in China to continue. We would love to hear from you and keep you informed as to the kingdom work taking place in China every day. Some say it is the last great frontier before the return of Jesus. What a privilege it is to play a role in that country's great awakening. Won't you join us?

If you would like information about ministry opportunities in China, please contact us at:

China Call, Inc.
P. O. Box 700515
Tulsa, OK 74170-0515
chcall@gorilla.net

ABOUT THE AUTHOR

Karen Hardin is a seasoned missionary who, along with her husband and three children, have ministered in Asia for the past fifteen years. Also a freelance writer, her work has appeared in *USA Today, Stories for the Spirit-Filled Believer, Blood and Thunder,* and *Charisma* magazine. Still actively  involved in minstry, Karen and her family make their home in Tulsa, Oklahoma.

ABOUT THE ARTIST

Nancy Harkins has excelled in painting and drawing since she was a young child and is primarily self-taught. Her watercolors have received awards in national and regional exhibitions and are in private and corporate collections around the country. They have been chosen for publication by the American Iris Society, Voice of the Martyrs Ministries, and North Light Books. She has also had the honor of showing her work at Gilcrease Museum in Tulsa, Oklahoma. She resides in Tulsa, with her husband and best friend, Ed.

Additional copies of this title
are available from your local bookstore.

Coming soon in the series:
Seasons of Love

If you have enjoyed this book,
we would love to hear from you!

Visit our website at:
www.whitestonebooks.com

*"...To him who overcomes I will give some of the hidden
manna to eat. And I will give him a white stone,
and on the stone a new name written which
no one knows except him who receives it."*
REVELATION 2:17 NKJV

WHITE STONE BOOKS
LAKELAND, FLORIDA